CAMPAIGN 336

STRASBOURG AD 357

The victory that saved Gaul

**RAFFAELE D'AMATO
& ANDREA FREDIANI**

ILLUSTRATED BY FLORENT VINCENT

Series editor Marcus Cowper

OSPREY PUBLISHING
Bloomsbury Publishing Plc
PO Box 883, Oxford, OX1 9PL, UK
1385 Broadway, 5th Floor, New York, NY 10018, USA
E-mail: info@ospreypublishing.com
www.ospreypublishing.com

OSPREY is a trademark of Osprey Publishing Ltd

First published in Great Britain in 2019

© Osprey Publishing Ltd, 2019

A catalogue record for this book is available from the British Library.

ISBN: PB: 978 1 4728 3398 3
          ePub: 978 1 4728 3397 6
          ePDF: 978 1 4728 3369 6
          XML: 978 1 4728 3399 0

19 20 21 22 23   10 9 8 7 6 5 4 3 2 1

Index by Angela Hall
Typeset in Myriad Pro and Sabon
Maps by Bounford.com
3D BEVs by The Black Spot
Page layouts by PDQ Digital Media Solutions, Bungay, UK
Printed in China through World Print Ltd.

Artist's note

For further information about Florent Vincent's work, please visit:

http://blog.armae.com/florent-vincent-illustrateur-historique.html

Osprey Publishing supports the Woodland Trust, the UK's leading woodland
conservation charity.

To find out more about our authors and books visit
www.ospreypublishing.com. Here you will find extracts, author
interviews, details of forthcoming events and the option to sign up for
our newsletter.

Authors' acknowledgements

The authors would like to express their gratitude to all the scholars, friends
and colleagues who supported this work. First of all to Dr Marina Mattei,
curator of the Capitolini Musei, Rome, who helped us to find the necessary
photographic material in various exhibitions and Italian museums. As
always Professor Livio Zerbini of Ferrara University has been vital in helping
obtain permission to view and photograph related material from different
museums and institutions.

Two further important and eminent people acknowledged here are Dr
Christian Miks, of the Römisch-Germanisches Zentralmuseum, Mainz,
Germany, whose photos and drawings of highly precious finds have
enriched this book. And last but not least, a special thank you to the curator
of the Coptic Department in the Hermitage, Dr Olga Osharina, who hosted
one of the authors in St Petersburg and supported his research.

Dr Massimo Bizzarri in Rome supported our work, as did Dr Andrei
Negin, who also contributed some of the splendid illustrations to this book.
Particular thanks also go to Andrea Salimbeti for his customary and valued
support with some of the illustrations, to Igor Dzis, and to Manfred Beer for
making his photographic archive available. A special thanks also to the
owners of several private collections who allowed their precious items to
be shown in this book.

The photos of the battlefield and of the important *stela* of Lepontius
appear thanks to the kindness of Dr Jasper Oorthuys and
Karwansaray Publishers.

Regarding the photographic images, we would like to thank the
following museums and institutions: the Germanisches Nationalmuseum,
Nürnberg; the Römische-Germanische Zentralmuseum, Mainz; the LVR-
Amt für Bodendenkmalpflege im Rheinland, Rheinisches Landesmuseum,
Trier; the Kunsthistorisches Museum, Vienna; the Musée Départemental
Arles Antique; the Musée d'histoire naturelle Guimet/Musée des
Confluences, Lyon; the Museo Diocesano of Acerenza, Italy; the Museo
storico dell'Arma del Genio, Rome; the Dipartimento dei beni culturali e
dell'identità siciliana, Sicily; the Hermitage Museum, St Petersburg;
Wikimedia Commons; and Heritage Auctions.

This book witnesses the first work for Osprey by the illustrator Florent
Vincent. The images and the details speak for themselves. Thank you,
Florent!

Dedication

Alla Nostra Alma Mater, Roma.

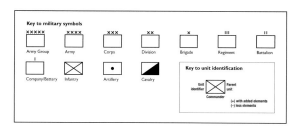

CONTENTS

ORIGINS OF THE CAMPAIGN   4

The Rhine frontier ∎ Constantine's dynasty ∎ The collapse in Gaul ∎ The arrival of Julian

CHRONOLOGY   16

THE APPROACH TO ARGENTORATUM   17

OPPOSING COMMANDERS   29

Roman ∎ Germanic

OPPOSING FORCES   33

Roman ∎ Germanic

OPPOSING PLANS   51

Germanic ∎ Roman

THE BATTLE OF ARGENTORATUM   56

AFTERMATH   80

Julian's follow-on operations ∎ The pacification of Gaul ∎ Emperor Julian

THE BATTLEFIELD TODAY   92

SELECT BIBLIOGRAPHY   93

INDEX   95

ORIGINS OF THE CAMPAIGN

Gaul (Gallia), even more than Africa, Dacia and Britannia, undoubtedly comprised one of the largest and longest-lasting conquests by the Romans, and the merit goes to Julius Caesar. Its resources and its rapid Romanization allowed the empire to prosper and rely on a geopolitical and economic nucleus beyond the confines of the Italian peninsula. Not by chance, it was only when the Gallic provinces, during the 5th century AD, began to see their territories shrink that the Western Roman Empire was no longer able to halt the decline and defend all its other borders. However, in the time period covered in this volume, the Romans knew how to deal with pressure along their borders consisting of raids, looting or, at most, temporary occupations of the frontier by enemy bands.

The Roman hero of the period under discussion, who led the defence of Gaul for five years, was a man who had never before taken a sword in his hand or fought an enemy on the battlefield. This man was Flavius Claudius Iulianus (Julian), at that time *caesar* over the Western provinces and then later *augustus* (emperor); he later became known as Julian the Apostate by his Christian enemies for his attempt to restore the ancient Pagan cults of Rome.

Roman soldiers hunting a boar and a deer, from a sarcophagus at Arelate (Arles), second half of 4th century AD. This sarcophagus, found in 1974 in the Trinquetaille area, shows how hunting was one of the preferred Roman methods for preparing for war. The presence of military belts and *fasciae crurales* (woollen socks laced up to the knee in a cross-garter pattern) mark these hunters as soldiers, probably in the retinue of a general. Note the fur collar worn without a cap, the *alicula*. (Musée Départemental Arles Antique, authors' photo, courtesy of the museum)

The Battle of Strasbourg (Argentoratum), fought in AD 357 between the Roman army under Julian and the confederation of Germanic tribes led by the Alemannic King Chnodomar, was the most striking military masterpiece of this extraordinary man, one of Rome's outstanding emperors. Although numerically inferior, Julian's army gained a complete victory by pushing the Alemanni beyond the Rhine and inflicting heavy casualties on them. The battle, one of the best documented military engagements of the 4th century AD, represented the culmination of the campaigns of Julian between 355 and 357 to drive the barbarians from Gaul and restore the line of Roman defensive fortifications along the Rhine, which had largely been destroyed during the civil war of AD 350–53. Julian himself wrote a book on the battle, which unfortunately remains lost to us, probably because of the *damnatio memoriae* suffered by Julian. There are three fundamental sources for the battle. Firstly, there is the account of Julian's personal historian, his contemporary Ammianus Marcellinus, who wrote his *Res Gestae* around AD 392. Secondly, there is Ammianus' teacher and friend of Julian, the orator Libanius, who wrote his account in AD 365 and thus is closer to the events. Thirdly, there is the account of the historian Zosimus, who wrote his *Historia Nova* in about AD 500. Ammianus has been often criticized by the modern historians, because he was an admirer of Julian and he celebrated his deeds. On the other hand, he was with Julian before the battle and, moreover, he collected additional information on it from his comrades and companion officers. Of course, a clear and complete reconstruction of what happened can only be obtained by reading Ammianus in conjunction with the other two sources and with the modern archaeology.

A Late Roman lord out hunting with soldiers and servants, Villa Romana del Tellaro, Sicily. (Dipartimento dei beni culturali e dell'identità siciliana; authors' photo)

THE RHINE FRONTIER

The tireless activity of Constantine the Great (AD 306–37), first as usurper, then as *caesar* and finally as *augustus*, restored a certain degree of stability on the Rhine frontier during the first half of the 4th century AD. A relative period of peace longer than any witnessed over the course of the previous century followed, although pressure continued from the Germanic tribes. The marked institutional and economic crisis into which the empire had fallen before the advent of Diocletian and the Tetrarchy, which witnessed 22 emperors across a 50-year timespan, had undermined Roman defensive emplacements along both its western and eastern borders. Whilst along the Euphrates Rome had to deal with the similarly structured kingdom of the Sassanid Persians, in Europe pressure was exerted by dozens of different tribes, occasionally acting as a confederation, but more often than not led by individual rulers who did not always respect any stipulated treaties (*foedera*) agreed with the current Roman emperor or his predecessors.

The rise of Constantine the Great, AD 306–24

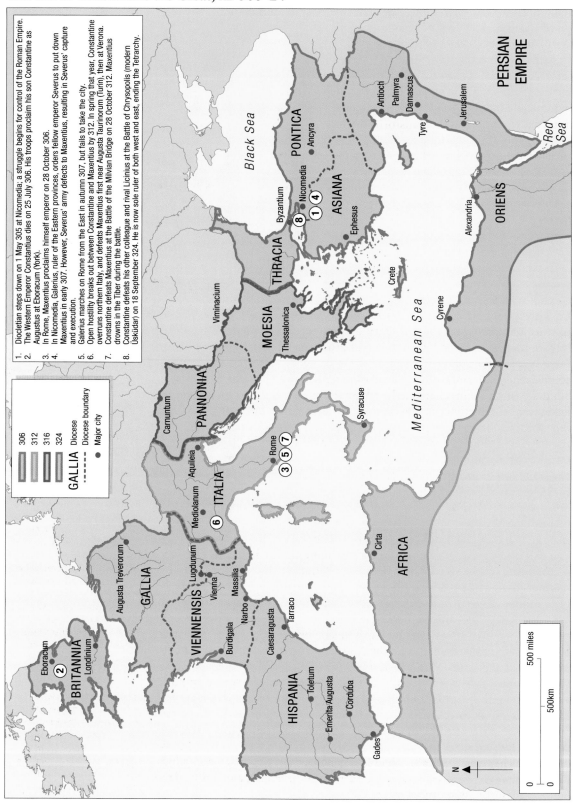

1. Diocletian steps down on 1 May 305 at Nicomedia; a struggle begins for control of the Roman Empire.
2. The Western Emperor Constantius dies on 25 July 306. His troops proclaim his son Constantine as Augustus at Eboracum (York).
3. In Rome, Maxentius proclaims himself emperor on 28 October 306.
4. In Nicomedia, Galerius, ruler of the Eastern provinces, orders fellow emperor Severus to put down Maxentius in early 307. However, Severus' army defects to Maxentius, resulting in Severus' capture and execution.
5. Galerius marches on Rome from the East in autumn 307, but fails to take the city.
6. Open hostility breaks out between Constantine and Maxentius by 312. In spring that year, Constantine overruns northern Italy, and defeats Maxentius first near Augusta Taurinorum (Turin), then at Verona.
7. Constantine defeats Maxentius at the Battle of the Milvian Bridge on 28 October 312. Maxentius drowns in the Tiber during the battle.
8. Constantine defeats his other colleague and rival Licinius at the Battle of Chrysopolis (modern Üsküdar) on 18 September 324. He is now sole ruler of both west and east, ending the Tetrarchy.

GALLIA Diocese
- - - - Diocese boundary
● Major city

306
312
316
324

PERSIAN EMPIRE

Red Sea

Black Sea

Mediterranean Sea

PONTICA
ASIANA
THRACIA
MOESIA
PANNONIA
ITALIA
GALLIA
VIENNENSIS
BRITANNIA
HISPANIA
AFRICA
ORIENS

Antioch
Palmyra
Damascus
Tyre
Jerusalem
Ancyra
Nicomedia
Byzantium
Ephesus
Alexandria
Crete
Cyrene
Thessalonica
Viminacium
Syracuse
Carnuntum
Aquileia
Rome
Mediolanum
Augusta Treverorum
Lugdunum
Vienna
Massilia
Narbo
Burdigala
Caesaragusta
Tarraco
Toletum
Emerita Augusta
Corduba
Gades
Cirta
Eboracum
Londinium

N

0   500 miles
0   500km

Rome's long-standing strategy had been to inflict exemplary defeats on her Germanic enemies and then incorporate any prisoners into the imperial army as auxiliary troops, or deporting them in order to repopulate deserted territories, making them *deviticii* (settlers), *laeti* (foreigners who were permitted to settle on Roman territory as long as they provided recruits for the Roman military) or *auxilia* (non-citizen Roman military). The aim was to transform them into allied populations settled along the empire's borders and acting as a forward line of defence against pressure from other more aggressive populations. The first documented *foedus* comes from the time of Marcus Aurelius – although the authenticity of the fragmentary evidence remains under discussion – between the Roman Empire and a band of barbarians, notably Vandals. While their families were held hostage by the Governor of Dacia, these barbarians fought against other ethnic groups, and their surviving members were allowed to settle in the territories in which rebellion had been eradicated. Over time, the barbarians were not only recruited into the auxiliary formations but also filled the manpower gaps that had appeared in the ranks of the legions, due to the increasing difficulties experienced by the authorities in sourcing recruits from within the empire. This changed the ethnic composition of these units, which became ever more varied, to the point that, by the 4th century AD, the term *barbarus* had become synonymous with 'soldier', and the allocation of military expenses had become known as the *fiscus barbaricus*.

Constantine had managed to tame the ambitions of the Franks by making them subject to Rome, but the Alemanni, another great confederation, remained under arms more often than they were at peace. The name itself (meaning 'all men') indicates their highly heterogeneous composition, which included tribes such as the Suebi, Quadi and Teutoni, who had played roles in previous conflicts between Romans and barbarians, and other lesser known ones such as the Charudes and Eudusii. The Alemanni originated from the aggregation of the tribes formed in Agri Decumates, the salient conquered by the Romans at the time of the Flavians to reduce the border area between the Rhine and the Danube, and the first emperor to confront them was Caracalla, who defeated them on the Main in AD 213. However, just half a century later they managed to push south of the Alps, as far as Mediolanum (Milan), before they were roundly defeated by Probus and forced to settle in the lands along the Neckar River. From that point onwards, they made repeated attempts to cross to the left bank of the Rhine, into Alsace, and into the territory around Lake Constance; their initial motives of capturing slaves and looting were subsequently replaced by the search for lands to be colonized. This was especially notable during the Roman civil wars, which sucked Roman military resources to the centre of the empire and stripped the frontier areas of military manpower.

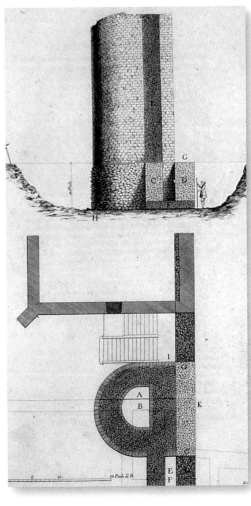

One of the Roman towers from the walls of Argentoratum (Strasbourg), by Silbermann, 1753. The third and final wall built at Argentoratum was made of sandstone. It was probably built in phases, at the end of 3rd or the beginning of the 4th century AD. It abutts directly to the earlier limestone wall. The new wall featured semi-circular towers spaced at 20–40m, with wider round towers at the four corners. Archaeological work has revealed a total of 17 semi-circular towers, whose diameters vary between 4.7m on the north-east section, 7.6m on the south-west section and 6.5m on the north-west section. The tower shown here no longer survives. (Public domain/Wikimedia Commons)

CONSTANTINE'S DYNASTY

Reconstruction of one of the helmets found at Koblenz (grave 1), with a Chi-ro christogram and metallic crest, dating from the second half of 4th century AD. From the time of Constantine the Great, many Christian soldiers displayed christograms on their weapons and armour. Constantius II was a deeply committed Arian Christian, continuing his father's policy of promoting Christians to the high offices of state. (Dr Christian Miks)

After the deep crisis of the 3rd century AD, the empire had recovered a precarious stability with the advent of Diocletian. Emerging victorious from the umpteenth civil war, and a usurper himself, the great emperor realized that the Roman Empire had become too big for a single man to succeed in stifling the ambitions of the provincial governors and to curb the pressure of the barbarians and the Persians. The empire was a territory extending thousands of miles from the Straits of Gibraltar to the Euphrates, from Hadrian's Wall to the Atlas Mountains. Therefore, Diocletian devised a complicated institution, known as the Tetrarchy, according to which four men – two emperors (*augusti*) and two deputy emperors or caesars (*caesari*) – ruled the empire. Diocletian and his colleague Maximianus would have been the *augusti*, with Constantius Chlorus and Galerius as the *caesari*; after 20 years, each *augustus* would retire and his *caesar* would take his place, accompanied by the election of two new *caesari*.

This new institution was inspired by the golden age of Rome, that of the Adoptive Emperors (the Nerva–Antonine Dynasty of AD 96–192), which had produced sovereigns such as Trajan, Hadrian, Antoninus Pius and Marcus Aurelius. The Nerva–Antonine Dynasty had worked because, in the absence of any direct heirs, each emperor had been forced to choose the best possible successor. During Diocletian's time, however, it was the direct heirs, who had been excluded from the succession, that undermined the system. Among them, the most skilful, ruthless and unscrupulous was Constantine who, excluded from the first succession despite being the son of the *augustus* Constantius Chlorus, took advantage of the premature death of his father to replace him and forced the other members of the new Tetrarchy to accept his status. Then he acted, plotted and began a series of wars that eliminated all his rivals and left him as sole administrator in the West while his brother-in-law Licinius, who had already been made *augustus* before him, ruled the East. But half of the Roman Empire was not enough for either of them and, after two further civil wars, in AD 324 Constantine emerged as the sole ruler of the Roman Empire.

Although under Diocletian and the Tetrarchy the empire had undergone important transformations especially in administrative, institutional and financial areas, Constantine imposed further deep-rooted changes to religious and military practices. In AD 313 in Milan, shortly after his victory over Maxentius at the Milvian Bridge, Licinius and Constantine issued an edict that confirmed the one issued by Galerius two years earlier, making the Christian religion *licita* (i.e. free to be practised); Christians had been fiercely persecuted by Diocletian and also by Galerius. From that point onwards, Constantine increasingly favoured the ecclesiastical hierarchy, to whom he granted privileges and tax advantages and made financial donations.

In the military field, Constantine completed the process of clearly differentiating between mobile and static forces, mainly located at key

Two golden *solidi*, the one on the left showing Constantius II, while the right-hand side coin depicts Julian. (Kunsthistorisches Museum, Vienna; authors' photo, courtesy of the museum)

points along the frontiers, through the distinction between the Limitanei or Ripuari (soldier-settlers anchored to a particular frontier territory) and the Comitatenses (forces quartered in cities). The latter formed the mobile troops who could accompany the emperor in a campaign or reach the most threatened sectors of the empire's frontier, in collaboration with the border troops. Under his rule, defeated barbarians were integrated into the army, offering many Germanic warriors the opportunity to forge a career in the imperial forces and even reach the highest command ranks. On the other hand, it must be remembered that it was an Alemannic king, Crocus, who raised Constantine up onto the shields of his warriors – the Auxilia of the army of Constantius Chlorus – and proclaimed him emperor in the aftermath of his father's death.

The succession of Constantine was simultaneously determined by dynastic needs and by the same administrative requirements that had led to the establishment of the Tetrarchy. It seems that the great emperor did not leave any precise instructions regarding the hierarchy, nor any rules relating to the government of the empire; at his death, in AD 337, Rome found itself with five rulers: his sons Constantine II, Constantius II and Constans, and his nephews Dalmatius and Hannibalianus. But the army in Constantinople, probably on the instigation of Constantius II, quickly got rid of the two nephews and left the empire in the hands of Constantine's three direct heirs. Only two children were spared the great purge in Byzantium that exterminated relatives and collaborators of the deceased emperor: Gallus and Julian (the former because he was unwell, the second because he was only a child). They were the sons of Constantine's half-brother, Julius Constans.

The tripartite division of the empire among the new *augusti*, however, did not endure for long. Constantine and Constans soon fell out and the former paid the price, falling in an ambush in AD 340 during an attempt to invade Italy, an area that was under his brother's control. From that moment, Constans, who was not yet 20 years old, assumed sovereignty over the entire West. Constantius, engaged in the East against Persia, could not challenge the land annexations that followed the death of his other brother. The young man proved to be a valiant general, and in the next ten years of his reign he achieved a series of victories against the barbarians who were pressing against the borders along the Rhine and in Britain. However, Constantius was a poor administrator, exacting and rapacious, scandalously immoral, and above all impatient with the demands of the army. This last point would have been enough to result in the fall of any emperor, and in the year AD 350 a

The Roman Empire, AD 337–53

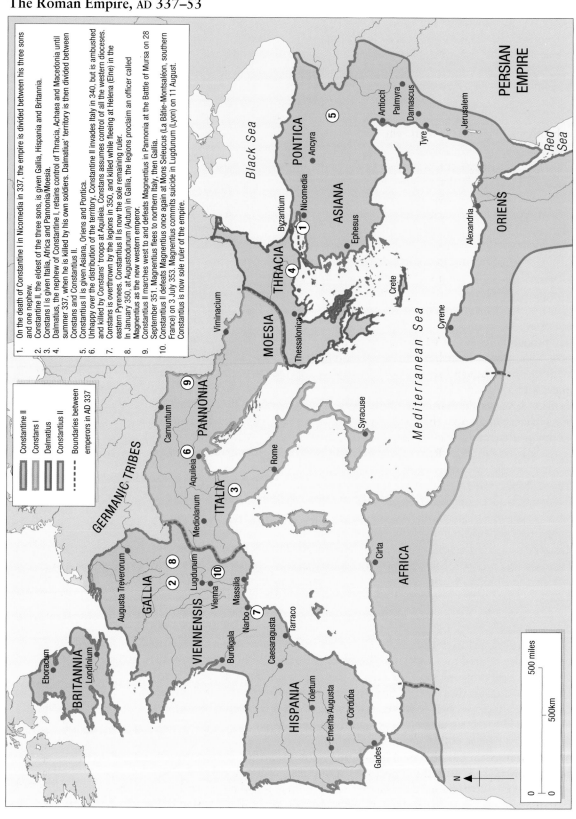

1. On the death of Constantine I in Nicomedia in 337, the empire is divided between his three sons and one nephew.
2. Constantine II, the eldest of the three sons, is given Gallia, Hispania and Britannia.
3. Constans I is given Italia, Africa and Pannonia/Moesia.
4. Dalmatius, the nephew of Constantine I, retains control of Thracia, Achaea and Macedonia until summer 337, when he is killed by his own soldiers. Dalmatius' territory is then divided between Constans and Constantius II.
5. Constantius II is given Asiana, Oriens and Pontica.
6. Unhappy over the distribution of the territory, Constantine II invades Italy in 340, but is ambushed and killed by Constans' troops at Aquileia. Constans assumes control of all the western dioceses.
7. Constans is overthrown by the legions in 350, and killed while fleeing at Helena (Elne) in the eastern Pyrenees. Constantius II is now the sole remaining ruler.
8. In January 350, at Augustodunum (Autun) in Gallia, the legions proclaim an officer called Magnentius as the new western emperor.
9. Constantius II marches west to and defeats Magnentius in Pannonia at the Battle of Mursa on 28 September 351. Magnentius flees to northern Italy, then Gallia.
10. Constantius II defeats Magnentius once again at Mons Seleucus (La Bâtie-Montsaléon, southern France) on 3 July 353. Magnentius commits suicide in Lugdunum (Lyon) on 11 August. Constantius is now sole ruler of the empire.

Constantine II
Constans I
Dalmatius
Constantius II
Boundaries between emperors in AD 337

conspiracy saw the purple cloth pass to a 47-year-old general, Flavius Magnus Magnentius, commander of the Legiones Palatinae of Jovians and Herculians in his role as Magister Militum Galliarum (Master of the Soldiers in Gaul).

Magnentius tried several times to come to an agreement with Constantius, but the emperor could not bring himself to share the empire with his brother's murderer, a man who was the son of a British slave and a Frankish warrior, and a pagan to boot. Constantine's son waited until the situation with the Sassanians had stabilized, and then, having appointed Gallus as *caesar* and delivered his sister Constantia into his care, moved westwards to face the usurper. The conflict culminated in the decisive Battle of Mursa Major in AD 351, on the Drava River, one of the most decisive in the history of Rome; over half of the 100,000 men involved remained in camp, and would have been put to better use in defending the borders from subsequent Germanic invasions in the west.

Although he emerged victorious from the battle, it took Constantius a further two years to rid himself of the usurper Magnentius, and soon circumstances would force him to do the same with his cousin Gallus. Magnentius committed suicide in AD 353, after a further defeat at the Battle of Mons Seleucus. Gallus was executed on the pretext that his rule over the Eastern provinces had been the most ferocious, unimaginative and insane of any despot, provoking famine, rebellion and murder throughout the Roman East. After his death, from Constantine's family there remained only Constantius and Julian, now in his early twenties, who had spent his life to date moving between Constantinople, Nicomedia and Cappadocia, immersed in studying classical authors, which had pushed him to abandon Christianity and to secretly rediscover the paganism of Roman tradition. Julian was verbose, superstitious, and committed to his interests; he seemed a harmless young man, too dedicated to his studies to pose a threat to Constantius, but at the same time too young and inexpert to be entrusted with an army for plugging the gaps that were appearing with increasing frequency along the western frontier.

THE COLLAPSE IN GAUL

After three years of civil war, the Rhine frontier had broken down. Along the Rhine, the situation was critical. Following the long crisis of the 3rd century AD, the Gallo-Roman cities had surrounded themselves with ramparts, which the barbarians rarely dared to besiege, lacking the necessary poliorcetic skills as well as the ability to manufacture siege engines. The borders, drained of soldiers by Magnentius for his war along the Danube against Constantius, was the object of continuous raiding: the Franks, as *laeti*, had taken possession of territories outside their jurisdiction, and the Alemanni had settled in the Rhine provinces. Some sources indicate that the

Paintings from the arcosolio (arched entombment) of Fl. Maximianus, Miles of a Numerus of Mattiarii Iuniores, second half of the 4th century AD, from the Catacombs of Villa Maria, Siracusa, Sicily. The name of the dead is recorded in the Tabula Inscriptionis painted over the grave: 'D(is) M(anibus). Fl(avius) Maximianus, de n(umero) Ma…a…s vi(xit) an(nos) XXI. Carinus frater pientissimus fecit' ('To the memory of the departed. Fl. Maximianus, of the Numerus of Ma…a…s (?), lived 21 years. His brother Carinus with great sorrow made this'. The symbology (crosses painted around him and on the Tabula Inscriptionis, peacocks and grapevine) reveals his Christian faith. Comparing the shield with those of the *Notitia Dignitatum*, Dr Jelusić has recently completed the inscription as follows: 'Dis Manibus, Flavius Maximianus de Numero Matiariorum iuniorum, vixit annos XXI Carinus Frater Pientissimus Fecit'. (Courtesy of the Pontificia Commissione di Archeologia Sacra, Ispettorato di Siracusa; authors' photo)

ABOVE LEFT
The remains of a Late Roman tower at Argentoratum (Strasbourg). In the late imperial period, the city walls were repaired with repurposed building stone (*spolia*), which often comprised carved funeral steles or fragments of inscriptions. This section of the walls lies in the basement of 47–49 rue des Grandes-Arcades (excavated in 1906 and listed as a Historic Monument in December 1920). (Public domain/Wikimedia Commons)

ABOVE RIGHT
The walls of Augustomagus (Senlis), begun at the end of the 3rd century AD but completed in the 4th, are one example of the transformation of Gallic cities into fortresses. Its walls featured 28 towers such as the one shown here. Cities were surrounded with walls up to 4m thick and 7–8m high (as here), to hold off barbarian raids. (Authors' photograph)

Alemanni were invited into Gaul by Constantius himself in order to hinder Magnentius. It is more likely, however, that they took advantage of the civil war to seize territories left without military control; a skilled administrator such as Constantius would never have entered into an agreement with the barbarians that risked damaging the empire. Indeed, Constantius rapidly moved against the Alemanni in the year following Magnentius' death, and ended his campaign of AD 354 by securing a number of peace and trade agreements with Germanic tribes, with very little actual fighting.

Constantius had appointed the Frank Silvanus, who had helped him secure victory at Mursa, to the office of Magister Peditum (commander of the infantry) in Gaul, and the general had proven his worth against the barbarians. However, it seems that several court intrigues pushed an already naturally suspicious Constantius to suspect he had been betrayed by Silvanus. With his back to the wall, the general risked it all by seizing power. Mirroring the fate of Magnentius, in August AD 355 he assumed the purple robes, only to be murdered by his own soldiers just 28 days later.

Without a coordinated defence, the Rhine front collapsed, and, according to the available sources, within a short period of time Franks, Alemanni and Saxons, driven by a ruthless leader called Chnodomar, sacked 45 cities including Colonia Agrippinensis (Cologne), destroyed defensive towers and fortresses, and enslaved a large number of inhabitants. Constantius had no choice: if he wanted to maintain even a token defence of the western frontier, while preventing a Roman commander from taking advantage of the situation to usurp power, he had to appoint a *caesar*, and the only surviving blood relative was Julian. He thus called upon his young cousin (who was only 24 years old) and, dragging him away from his philosophy studies, dispatched him to Gaul as his representative.

Julian assumed the purple on 6 November AD 355 in Mediolanum (Milan), where he married Constantius' daughter Elena, and then departed as *caesar* for Gaul on 1 December that same year. His designated role as *caesar*, and not as supreme commander, was due to the fact that Constantius instinctively distrusted him, and also, objectively, because Julian had almost no military experience. Julian was thus relegated to the role of lieutenant beneath the Magister Peditum Marcellus, who had succeeded Silvanus. The latter intended to use Julian as a representative of the imperial family, or rather, as Julian himself wrote, 'as a puppet who carried his portrait'.

Reconstruction of Castellum Divitia, 4th century AD. Castellum Divitia was a Roman military camp, built between AD 308 and 315 on the eastern bank of the Rhine, adjacent to the former legionary fortress of Colonia Agrippinensis, in order to create a 'bridgehead' that would protect against raids by the neighbouring Frankish tribes. It was located in modern Deutz. The fort's sides measured 142.35m, and the walls were about 3.3m high, while the external towers protruded up to 4.06m. The whole site occupied an area of 2.25 hectares, while the internal area covered 1.81 hectares. At about 30m from the walls of the fortress a large ditch 12m wide and 3m deep has been excavated. There were only two gateways into the fort (usually there were four entrances), each flanked by a pair of towers protecting the bridge. A further 10 towers were situated along the walls and at the corners, projecting outwards. Its dimensions suggest that no fewer than 900 men populated this *castellum*. (Museo storico dell'Arma del genio, Rome; authors' photo, courtesy of the museum)

THE ARRIVAL OF JULIAN

On his arrival in Julia Viennensis (Vienne), where he would diligently spend the winter in the practice of arms and in studying the deeds and tactics of the great leaders of antiquity, Julian found a disastrous situation. The Franks had extended their hegemony over all of Toxandria (the Brabant), and the Alemanni now held the entire Alsace region, controlling the territories of cities like Argentoratum (Strasbourg), Brocomagus (Brumath), Tres Tabernae (Saverne), Saliso (Seltz), Noviomagus (Speyer), Borgogetomagus (Worms) and Mogontiacum (Mainz), while refusing to settle within their walls. According to Ammianus, who participated in this first campaign of Julian as an officer, to them cities were like graveyards surrounded by gates. Constantius had succeeded in AD 354 in entering into a peace treaty with two of their rulers, Gundomadus and Vadomarus, but not with the more aggressive Chnodomar, the thorn in Magnentius' side; the situation was rendered more explosive by the stragglers of the usurper's army, who were living by raiding and pillaging.

Julian himself described the situation thus, in his *Letter to the Senate and People of Athens* (p.269):

> And the Barbarians then controlled on our side of the Rhine the whole country that extends from its sources to the ocean. Moreover those who were settled nearest to us were as much as three hundred stades from the banks of the Rhine, and a district three times as wide they had with their raids converted into a desert, so that the Gauls could not even pasture their cattle there. Then too there were certain cities deserted by their inhabitants, near which the barbarians were not encamped.

From AD 356, Constantius took direct control of operations. This campaign, according to the emperor's intentions, would act as a display of military power that would compel the Alemanni to carry out a bloodless withdrawal back across the Rhine. He planned to march against the barbarians from Raetia, while Julian was tasked with closing off the escape routes from Gaul. To do this, the *caesar* first went to Augustodunum (Autun), then to Durocorturum (Reims), where he joined the bulk of Marcellus' army. His first military act of personal initiative did not go well, and seemed to confirm

Julian's campaign in Gaul, AD 356

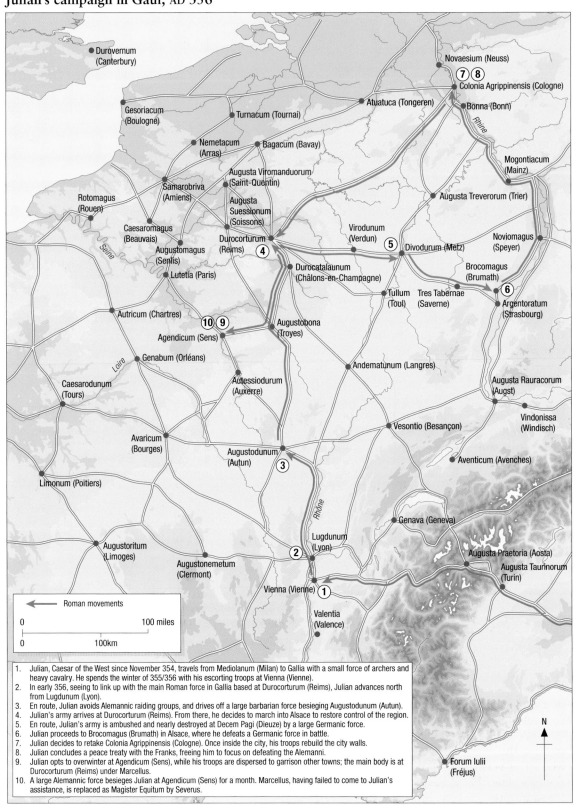

1. Julian, Caesar of the West since November 354, travels from Mediolanum (Milan) to Gallia with a small force of archers and heavy cavalry. He spends the winter of 355/356 with his escorting troops at Vienna (Vienne).
2. In early 356, seeing to link up with the main Roman force in Gallia based at Durocorturum (Reims), Julian advances north from Lugdunum (Lyon).
3. En route, Julian avoids Alemannic raiding groups, and drives off a large barbarian force besieging Augustodunum (Autun).
4. Julian's army arrives at Durocorturum (Reims). From there, he decides to march into Alsace to restore control of the region.
5. En route, Julian's army is ambushed and nearly destroyed at Decem Pagi (Dieuze) by a large Germanic force.
6. Julian proceeds to Brocomagus (Brumath) in Alsace, where he defeats a Germanic force in battle.
7. Julian decides to retake Colonia Agrippinensis (Cologne). Once inside the city, his troops rebuild the city walls.
8. Julian concludes a peace treaty with the Franks, freeing him to focus on defeating the Alemanni.
9. Julian opts to overwinter at Agendicum (Sens), while his troops are dispersed to garrison other towns; the main body is at Durocorturum (Reims) under Marcellus.
10. A large Alemannic force besieges Julian at Agendicum (Sens) for a month. Marcellus, having failed to come to Julian's assistance, is replaced as Magister Equitum by Severus.

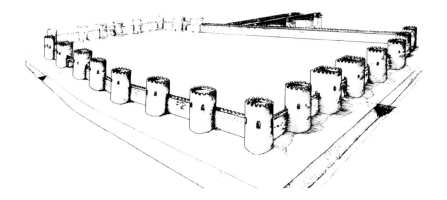

A reconstruction of the Late Roman fortifications of Koblenz. The military importance of the city (known to the Romans as Castellum apud Confluentes) in the defences of Germania Superior is attested to by the large number of helmets and shield bosses found there, and by the imposing fortifications erected during the 4th century AD. (Andrea Salimbeti, after Miks)

the doubts Constantius had towards him. Against the advice of the generals that Constantius had placed around him, he attacked the Alemanni in Decem Pagi (Dieuze). But the thick fog and his lack of familiarity with the area resulted in the fragmentation of the various units of his army, and two rear-guard legions were assailed by the barbarians who, taking advantage of their better local knowledge, circumvented the Roman camp and surprised it from behind. Only the clashing of arms and the soldiers' shouts alerted the rest of the army to the attack and directed them to help their comrades, avoiding a massacre along the lines of the Teutoburg Forest in AD 9. In contrast, the Romans had good fortune during the transfer to Brocomagus, where a group of Alemanni blocked Julian's way forward. He charged them using the wings of his army in a concave/crescent formation – a 'pincer manoeuvre' as Ammianus calls it (*Res Gestae* XVI, 2,12–13) – and secured a rapid victory. This encounter was not a decisive one, but because Constantius was now in their territories, it was enough to induce the barbarians to seek a truce. This allowed Julian to return to the north and take care of the Franks, fortifying Colonia Agrippinensis (Cologne), from where he left for winter quarters at Agendicum (Sens), having strengthened the peace agreements with the Frankish kings.

Reflecting on his first campaigning episode, the young *caesar* did not feel satisfied. His youthful ambition, which had long awaited an opportunity to free himself from the confines imposed on him by his cousin and from his reputation as a 'bookworm' due to his studies, could not consider it a brilliant military campaign as it lacked decisive events, and he had suffered at least one defeat. But the chance to prove his ability to learn quickly came sooner than expected. The lack of provisions led him to reduce the number of forces that he garrisoned at Agendicum (Sens). Elite troops, like the Scholae Palatinae, the Scutarii and the Gentiles (barbarians mainly composed of Sarmatians and Taifali), that constituted his bodyguard, were distributed among the various fortresses, and the reduced numbers remaining in the city were enough to push the Alemanni to seek glory besieging the stronghold. But after a month of fruitless attacks, the barbarians were forced to cease and withdraw. The siege of Agendicum (Sens) was the keystone of Julian's military career. It increased his influence among his soldiers, who had seen him day and night, actively coordinating the defence, and at the same time reduced the esteem in which Marcellus was held by Constantius. Although Marcellus was close by during the siege, he failed to move for its entire duration, possibly believing that he was doing a favour to the emperor, or because he detested the independent and enterprising young *caesar*.

CHRONOLOGY

331   6 November: Julian is born in Constantinople, the second son of Julius Constantius, brother of Constantine the Great.

337   Julian's family is exterminated by the Palatine Guards of Constantine's sons in Constantinople.

340   Spring: Constantine II is killed in an ambush during his attempt to seize power; his brothers, Constans and Constantius II, rule the Western and Eastern parts of the empire respectively.

350   Constans is murdered by the usurper Magnentius at Autun (Augustodunum) in Gaul.

351   Having defeated Magnentius at the Battle of Mursa, Constantius II becomes the sole ruler of the Roman Empire. Profiting from the Roman civil wars, Franks and Alemanni cross the Rhine border.

354   September: Gallus, Julian's brother, is executed by direct order of Constantius II.

355   1 December: following his appointment as *caesar*, Julian departs for Gaul from Mediolanum (Milan) accompanied by 360 troops.

356   August: Julian retakes Colonia Agrippinensis (Cologne) from the Alemanni, and is then besieged by barbarians in his winter quarters at Agendicum (Sens).

357   Julian assumes supreme command of all the troops in Gaul.

       15 (or 25) August: Battle of Argentoratum (Strasbourg). Julian, commanding 13,000 men, defeats Chnodomar's 35,000-strong confederation, who have been crossing the Rhine for the past three days. Only 243 Romans are killed compared to 6,000 Germanic warriors.

358–59 Julian pacifies Toxandria (the Brabant) destroying an army of Frankish Salii at Atuatuca (Tongeren) and defeating the Chamavi located on the other side of the Mesa (Moselle) River, on the lower Rhine.

360   February: Julian is proclaimed *Augustus* by his troops in Lutetia (Paris).

Late Roman *fibulae* (brooches), second half of the 4th century AD. The left *fibula* is a flat-headed example, while the centre and the right examples are parts of the typical 'crossbow' *fibula* design in this period. One comes from the territory of Mogontiacum (Mainz); the provenance of the other two is unknown, but they are probably from the Rhine area. (Römisch-Germanisches Zentralmuseum; author's photo, courtesy of the museum)

THE APPROACH TO ARGENTORATUM

During the winter of AD 356/357, while headquartered at Agendicum (Sens), Julian gathered recruits in every way possible, from allied tribes and the young available for military service. He trained them for a new campaign in AD 357, which according to Constantius' plans would form a pincer operation against the Alemanni, who were considered 'mere wild beasts, accustomed to living off robbery'. The intention of the campaign was to 'squeeze [the Alemanni] into a narrow space by a pincer movement ... and cut them to pieces', thereby relieving the Gallo-Romans from barbarian 'slaughter, pillage and fire' (Ammianus, XV, 5,2; XVI, 11.3).

According to the instructions of the emperor, who was about to leave for the Danubian border, his cousin Julian would continue to operate in the north with his 13,000 soldiers; the southern front, however, would be assigned to the new Magister Peditum Barbatio, who was at Augusta Vindelicorum (Augsburg) with at least 25,000 troops. While Barbatio would cross the Rhine from the south, Julian's army would prevent the enemy's retreat. One of the key objectives of the imperial plan was to have two armies meeting on opposite sides of the Rhine south of Strasbourg in order to construct a bridge. This bridge was to have served two important functions. In addition to expanding Roman military presence along the Rhine border region, it

A small section of a late Roman sleeve from a tunic. (Musée des Confluences, Lyon; authors' photo, courtesy of the museum)

The Roman pincer plan, AD 357

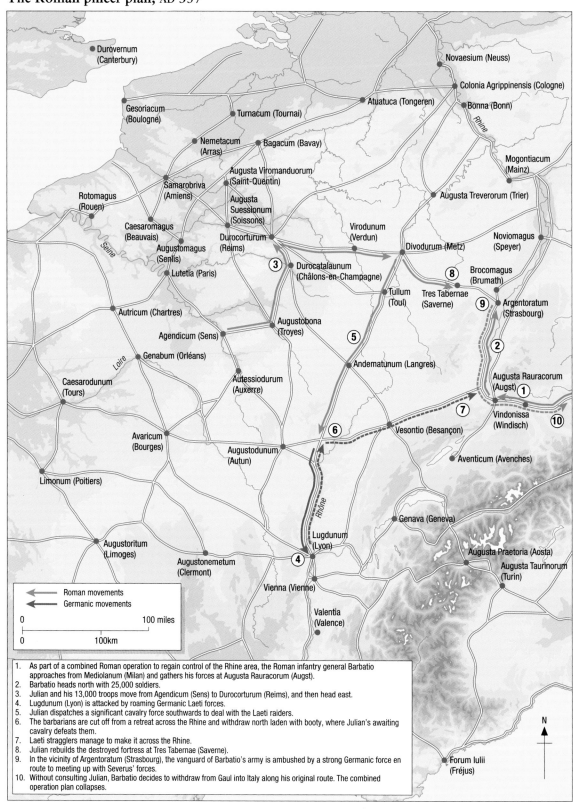

Durovernum (Canterbury)
Gesoriacum (Boulogne)
Turnacum (Tournai)
Atuatuca (Tongeren)
Novaesium (Neuss)
Colonia Agrippinensis (Cologne)
Bonna (Bonn)
Nemetacum (Arras)
Bagacum (Bavay)
Augusta Viromanduorum (Saint-Quentin)
Samarobriva (Amiens)
Rotomagus (Rouen)
Augusta Suessionum (Soissons)
Mogontiacum (Mainz)
Augusta Treverorum (Trier)
Caesaromagus (Beauvais)
Augustomagus (Senlis)
Durocorturum (Reims)
Virodunum (Verdun)
Divodurum (Metz)
Noviomagus (Speyer)
Lutetia (Paris)
Durocatalaunum (Châlons-en-Champagne)
Tullum (Toul)
Tres Tabernae (Saverne)
Brocomagus (Brumath)
Argentoratum (Strasbourg)
Autricum (Chartres)
Augustobona (Troyes)
Agendicum (Sens)
Genabum (Orléans)
Andematunum (Langres)
Augusta Rauracorum (Augst)
Caesarodunum (Tours)
Autessiodurum (Auxerre)
Avaricum (Bourges)
Augustodunum (Autun)
Vesontio (Besançon)
Vindonissa (Windisch)
Aventicum (Avenches)
Limonum (Poitiers)
Genava (Geneva)
Augustoritum (Limoges)
Augustonemetum (Clermont)
Lugdunum (Lyon)
Augusta Praetoria (Aosta)
Augusta Taurinorum (Turin)
Vienna (Vienne)
Valentia (Valence)
Forum Iulii (Fréjus)
Seine · **Loire** · **Rhine** · **Rhône**

Roman movements
Germanic movements

0   100 miles
0   100km

N

1. As part of a combined Roman operation to regain control of the Rhine area, the Roman infantry general Barbatio approaches from Mediolanum (Milan) and gathers his forces at Augusta Rauracorum (Augst).
2. Barbatio heads north with 25,000 soldiers.
3. Julian and his 13,000 troops move from Agendicum (Sens) to Durocorturum (Reims), and then head east.
4. Lugdunum (Lyon) is attacked by roaming Germanic Laeti forces.
5. Julian dispatches a significant cavalry force southwards to deal with the Laeti raiders.
6. The barbarians are cut off from a retreat across the Rhine and withdraw north laden with booty, where Julian's awaiting cavalry defeats them.
7. Laeti stragglers manage to make it across the Rhine.
8. Julian rebuilds the destroyed fortress at Tres Tabernae (Saverne).
9. In the vicinity of Argentoratum (Strasbourg), the vanguard of Barbatio's army is ambushed by a strong Germanic force en route to meeting up with Severus' forces.
10. Without consulting Julian, Barbatio decides to withdraw from Gaul into Italy along his original route. The combined operation plan collapses.

A gold 'crossbow' *fibula* (brooch) bearing the inscription IVLIANE VIVAS. (Kunsthistorisches Museum, Vienna; authors's photo, courtesy of the museum)

would expedite the withdrawal of Alemanni settlers out of Gaul. But the complex movement, which provided for a convergence of the two columns towards the barbarians of the upper and middle Rhine, was marred by the hostility that the new commander of the infantry, one of Gallus' killers, held towards Julian. And so it was that, at the first unforeseen event, the plan shipwrecked miserably.

The unforeseen manifested itself in the form of unidentified barbarians, which Ammianus simply calls Laeti (XVI, 11.4), a ruthless tribe skilled in seasonal raiding. This description by Ammianus fits well with that of the author of the *Panegyrici Latini* VIII (21.1) who said that the Laeti were a barbarian tribe or a grouping similar to the Franks. We know from other parts of Ammianus' work that these Laeti were a tribal unit independent of Roman authority, though settled within the riverine frontier of the later Western empire. He records a letter to Constantius as follows: 'I will furnish Spanish horses for your chariots, and to be added to the household troops of Gentiles and the Scutarii some young men of the Laeti, a tribe of barbarians on this side of the Rhine, or at any rate from those of them who voluntarily come over to us. And this I promise to do to the end of my life, with not only a willing but an eager spirit.'

These Laeti tribesmen, who were probably rebellious colonists, infiltrated themselves between the two arms of the pincer movement and tried to storm Lugdunum (Lyon). However, once it was clear that the enterprise was beyond their means, they began to plunder the surrounding territory. Julian sent three squadrons of light cavalry (*tres cunei equitum expeditorum*), who managed to defeat and put the enemy to flight; but some survivors managed to bypass Barbatio's camp and crossed the Rhine unmolested. According to Ammianus (XVI, 11), this was 'because Bainobaudes [tribune of the Scola Scutatiorum] and Valentinian ... who along with the cavalry troops they commanded had been ordered to attend to that matter, were forbidden by Cella, tribune of the Scutarii, who had come to the campaign as Barbatio's colleague, to watch

JULIAN PREPARES THE AUXILIA PALATINA OF THE CORNUTI SENIORES FOR THEIR RAID AGAINST THE GERMANS (PP. 20–21)

In locations where conventional methods of fighting the enemy were less effective, Roman auxiliaries could also employ irregular ones. And so it was that in summer AD 357, during his campaign against the Alemanni who had settled in the bend of the Rhine, Julian, who could not cross the river using a pontoon bridge because he was lacked the necessary vessels, 'with words of encouragement sent the light-armed auxiliaries with [the Frank] Bainobaudes, Tribune of the Cornuti, to perform a memorable feat … and they, now wading through the shallows, now swimming on their shields, which they put under them like canoes, came to a neighbouring island and landing there they butchered everyone they found, men and women alike, without distinction of age, like so many sheep' (Ammianus XVI, 11.9).

Here we see the *caesar* Julian (**1**) and the tribune Bainobaudes (**2**) preparing the *auxilia* soldiers for their attack. The reconstruction of Julian's equipment and dress is based on his coinage, statues and from the contemporary mosaics of the Villa Romana del Tellaro in Sicily. The appearance of the Auxilia Palatina of the Cornuti (**3**, **4**, **5** and **6**) has been reconstructed from the Arch of Constantine and from archaeological finds from the age of Julian. Note the method of storing the *plumbatae* (lead-weighted throwing darts) on the shield's interior (**7**) and the typical totemic symbol of the Cornuti depicted on their shields (**8**) or on their helmets (**9**).

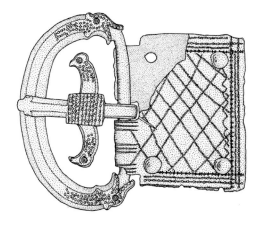

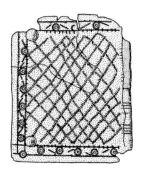

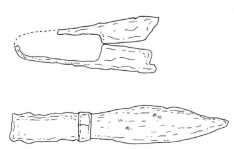

Items from a soldier's grave (no. 111) at Oudenburg, Belgium, dating from the second half of the 4th century AD. The bronze buckle (top left) features animal protomes, and measures 7.2cm long and 4.61–5.37cm wide. The bronze belt fitting (top right) measures 5cm x 4.34cm. The two lower items comprise (left) iron scissors (15cm long), a knife (bottom left) with wooden grip (24.5cm long) and a gilded crossbow brooch in bronze (7.4cm long). (Andrea Salimbeti, after Sommer)

the road over which they were informed that the Germans would return.' Although victorious, the enthusiastic Julian had lost time with this operation.

A series of recriminations began between the two commanders, and Barbatio justified himself by stating that the two tribunes to which Julian had entrusted the operations, Bainobaudes and Valentinian – the future emperor – had invaded his area of operations and attempted to move the soldiers against him. But soon Barbatio would have to account for other disasters to the emperor. Faced with the approaching army of Julian from Durocorturum (Reims), where the *caesar* had gathered his troops, the Alemanni had blocked the Col de Saverne pass with large tree trunks and found refuge on the islets that dotted the Rhine; they considered themselves so secure there that 'with wild and mournful cries they heaped insults upon the Romans and Caesar'. Julian decided to build a pontoon bridge to teach them a lesson, and asked Barbatio to supply seven vessels; but it seems that the commander of the infantry preferred to burn all the ships at his disposal rather than send them to Julian (Ammianus, XVI, 11.8).

Julian, however, found another way to reach these small islands. It was summer, and the level of the river had dropped to the point of allowing it to be forded. A company of lightly armed *auxilia* (perhaps from the Cornuti), led by Bainobaudes, reached the island nearest to the left bank, where the Romans killed the men, women and children they encountered there. The soldiers then helped themselves to some boats on the island and continued their work on those nearby, returning to shore only when they could kill no more, and when they had accumulated all the loot they could carry. Some of the occupied islands escaped their attention, but the barbarians who occupied them chose to vacate them anyway (Ammianus, XVI, 11.9).

A Late Roman Pannonian cap, found in Leens, Leiden, c. AD 400. Although the date of this object remains unclear, its shape and size corresponds perfectly to the 'pillbox' type known as *pileus pannonicus* worn by Late Roman soldiers under the helmet, or on its own, as shown in many illustrations and described by Vegetius. (Robbert Jan Looman/National Museum of Antiquities, Leiden)

Nevertheless, Barbatio continued to hinder Julian. The Col de Saverne north-west of Strasbourg connected the Pforzheim Pass, in the Black Forest, with the pass that allowed the crossing of the Vosges Mountains, and represented the preferred access route for the Alemanni into Gaul. Julian's next move therefore was to guard it and fortify it. Barbatio refused to send him supplies, burning those he did not consider necessary for supporting his own troops. Julian, in response, put his men to gathering wheat from the crops sown by the barbarians (who were already settling on the left bank of the Rhine) in order to stockpile food for the defenders of the fortress of Tres Tabernae (Saverne) for a whole year. By now, however, rumours had begun to spread that Julian had been sent to Gaul by Constantius to make a fool of him or even to have him killed in the fighting.

It was Barbatio instead who was subjected to ridicule, when, surprised by a horde of Alemanni, he opted to flee, abandoning his supply train to them. He then withdrew his troops to Augusta Rauracorum (Augst), where he quartered them before returning to Italy, behaving as if he had successfully concluded his expedition. Libanius (*Funeral Oration for Julian*, XVIII, 49–51) writes that the Alemanni sent logs down the Rhine and destroyed the unfinished Roman bridge. Both commanders wrote to the emperor to give their version of events, which led to Constantius recalling Barbatio and stripping him of command.

With the unexpected defeat of Barbatio, Julian found himself alone facing a multitude of barbarians, and with responsibility for hundreds of miles of border. In addition, the Magister Peditum had taken away his 25,000 men, so Julian had to face the enemy with only 13,000–15,000 (at best) soldiers. News of the relatively thin forces at the disposal of the *caesar* reached the

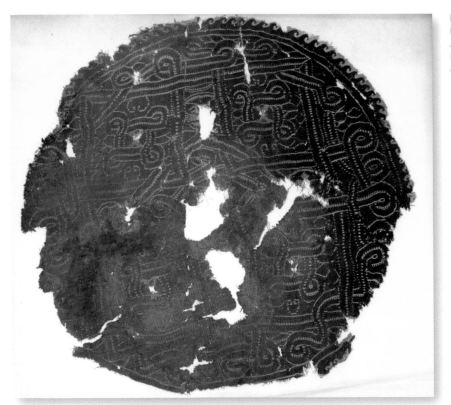

Embroidery (*orbiculus*) on a Late Roman tunic, 4th century AD. (Musée des Confluences, Lyon; authors' photo, courtesy of the museum)

barbarians by means of a deserter from the forces of the Magister Peditum, and this led the Alemanni to decide to unite their forces, hitherto deeply divided, to inflict a definitive blow on Julian. The ever-willing Chnodomar, exploiting the opportunity presented by Barbatio's sudden withdrawal, succeeded in forming an alliance of his fellow kings Vestralpus, Urius, Ursicinus, Serapio, Suomarius and Hortarius. Moreover, of the two former allies of the Romans, Gundomadus had been assassinated, and part of the tribe of Vadomarus had opted to join the coalition.

The Alemannic forces crossed the Rhine and assembled just north of Argentoratum (Strasbourg). The Germanic forces took the field on the left of the Rhine, north-west of the city, along the road leading to Saverne, between two Roman fortresses in the territory of the Triboci, Tribunci and Concordia (the precise location is hard to determine). According to the *Itinerarium Antonini* (a Roman roadbook) the latter was exactly halfway between Brocomagus (Brumath) and Noviomagus (Speyer), perhaps Altenstadt near Wissembourg, while the former has been identified with Saliso (Seltz) or with Lauterbourg.

Julian's poor reputation as a leader induced the barbarians to order the *caesar* to vacate territory that they considered to be rightly their own. From Chnodomar's perspective, Barbatio's withdrawal could have been interpreted as a sign of Constantius' unwillingness to wage war, and therefore a confirmation of earlier settlement agreements between the Alemanni and the *augustus*. It has been put forward by modern historians that the reaction of the Alemanni was merely due to Julian's aggressive policy. However, it is clear from Ammianus' account that Chnodomar used this as an excuse to achieve what he had long sought, the creation of an Alemannic kingdom

The approach to Argentoratum, August AD 357

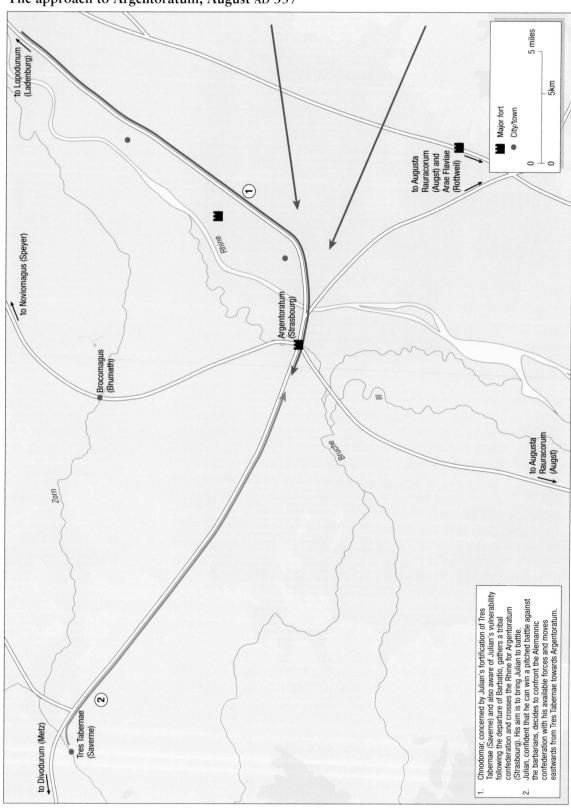

to Lopodunum
(Ladenburg)

to Augusta
Rauracorum
(Augst) and
Arae Flaviae
(Rottweil)

Rhine

to Noviomagus (Speyer)

Argentoratum
(Strasbourg)

Brocomagus
(Brumath)

Zorn

Ill

Bruche

to Augusta
Rauracorum
(Augst)

to Divodurum (Metz)

Tres Tabernae
(Saverne)

Major fort
City/town

0   5 miles

0   5km

1. Chnodomar, concerned by Julian's fortification of Tres Tabernae (Saverne) and also aware of Julian's vulnerability following the departure of Barbatio, gathers a tribal confederation and crosses the Rhine for Argentoratum (Strasbourg). His aim is to bring Julian to battle.
2. Julian, confident that he can win a pitched battle against the barbarians, decides to confront the Alemannic confederation with his available forces and moves eastwards from Tres Tabernae towards Argentoratum.

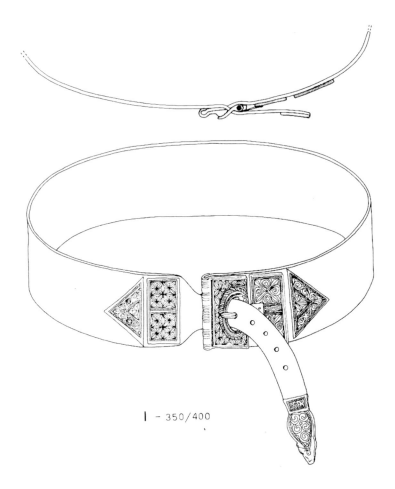

Reconstruction of a Late Roman belt in the Kerbschnitt style, from the second half of the 4th century AD. (Andrea Salimbeti, after Milano: Capitale dell'Impero)

I − 350/400

in Gaul. 'But [Julian], a stranger to fear, neither lost his temper nor felt aggrieved, but laughing at the presumption of the savages, he detained the envoys until the work of fortification was ended and remained steadfast in the same attitude of resolution' (Ammianus, XVI, 12.3).

Julian decided to advance and fight a pitched battle. His decision can be considered one of the key choices in the history of the Roman Empire. For an inexperienced general like him, it would have been reasonable to await the enemy, apparently with a clear numerical superiority, sheltering behind his fortifications – a passive strategy that, sooner or later, would probably have compromised Rome's positions along the Rhine frontier. However, Julian was imbued with reading ancient classical texts, in which Livy, Polybius and Caesar himself recounted the exploits of Rome's greatest leaders. If he had not learned how to win on a battlefield from them, he had at least drawn spirit from these leaders, whose example and determination to succeed had always allowed the Romans to overcome the most desperate situations and the most impossible challenges.

According to Ammianus (XVI, 12.60), the decision to fight was an act of bravery against all the odds. It was also an act of personal liberation and political defiance aimed at the emperor Constantius. The evidence from our sources suggests that Julian did not want to avoid conflict. For Julian, the restoration of Gaul and the defeat of the Alemanni were not the only goals; he also sought to offer a response to Constantius' behaviour (as he himself wrote in his *Letter to the Athenians*, p.273, stating that the emperor was 'too accustomed to providing for the Barbarians'). Moreover, the Germanic settlements west of the Rhine remained a thorn in Rome's side. Not only were they a political embarrassment for the *augustus*, but they left Italy, the ancestral core of the empire, exposed and vulnerable. Furthermore, the peace treaties Constantius offered the Alemanni at the end of AD 354 were poorly received by the legions, who felt both insulted and cheated.

With the ancient Roman leaders to inspire him, Julian convinced his army not to wait for the enemy behind the strong fortifications of Tres Tabernae but to face the barbarians in the open, at a place 21 miles away. At dawn on 14 (or possibly 24) August AD 357, the army set off, with the infantry in two columns in the centre, protected along its flanks by the cavalry, among which the Catafractarii and the Sagittarii were prominent, following first the military road to Brocomagus (Brumath), then the main between Argentoratum (Strasbourg) and Mogontiacum (Mainz).

Towards midday, with the enemy almost in sight, perhaps near Wintzenheim-Kochersberg, 12 miles from Tres Tabernae, Julian recalled the vanguard, gathered his men and analyzed the situation. The spectrum of the Teutoburg Forest was ever-present in the minds of all Roman commanders, including the young *caesar*, gazing before him at the tortuous paths that disappeared into the woods and then at a plain scorched by the August heat. Julian ordered his troops to set up a fortified camp, refresh themselves, gather their forces and give battle only at dawn the following day. But the soldiers 'gnashed and ground their teeth and showed their eagerness for battle by striking their spears and shields together, and besought him that they might be led against an enemy who was already in sight, trusting in the favour of God in Heaven, in their own self-confidence, and in the tried valour of their lucky general'. The officers themselves, whose opinion was voiced by the Praefectus Praetorii Galliae, Flavius Florentius, considered it more appropriate not to delay battle, taking advantage of the fact that the enemy was still united, and therefore easier to target with cavalry charges and arrowshot. A delay, Flavius argued, would allow the barbarians to scatter, and the Roman soldiers would be left with the impression that a guaranteed victory had been wrested from their hands (Ammianus XVI, 12.14).

Julian was persuaded to continue: he had not yet fought a field battle and his position was still far from secure. The junior officers were able to influence him and to assert their greater experience, but the result of the imminent clash would change everything: the *caesar* would emerge from it aware of his full potential and convinced he had been chosen by the gods to reintroduce Rome to the glories of the past.

After a further three miles of marching, Julian's army arrived on a hilltop (possibly modern Hurtigheim, less than 16km from the Rhine), where four Alemannic lookouts were stationed. Three managed to escape on horseback in time, but one, who attempted to flee on foot, was captured by the Romans. The latter learned from him that the barbarians had taken 72 hours to cross the Rhine, and Julian was informed of the strength of the Germanic host. While crossing a hill near Argentoratum (Strasbourg), the Romans observed the Alemanni forming their bands into battle array. The imperial army clearly enjoyed an unquestionable strategic advantage: in case of difficulty, it could always fall back into the fortifications at Tres Tabernae, while the Alemanni had only the Rhine to their rear.

OPPOSING COMMANDERS

ROMAN

From the time of the earliest Church Fathers, **Julian,** in an attempt to discredit him, has been known as the Apostate. Others, keen to praise him, have dubbed him the Philosopher. Polymnia Athanassiadi-Fowden describes Julian as a loyal defender of the empire, pure in faith and motivation. This great lover of letters, once he had been proclaimed emperor, decided to restore the pagan cults of his own free will according to his own cultural preferences. As emperor, it was his right to do so. He was an exalted man, who mostly acted in good faith, who sometimes acted precipitously, notably in the eastern part of the empire from which he originated. Although his Mithraic eclecticism sometimes triumphed over him, it must be admitted that his actions mostly turned out to be ineffectual and relatively utopian in nature. He was the last great emperor of a unified Rome.

Elevated to the purple in Mediolanum (Milan) in AD 355 (aged 25), and proclaimed *Augustus* by his own soldiers in Lutetia (Paris) in AD 360, he was recognized as the sole emperor in AD 361 and remained so until his death 20 months later near Ctesiphon during his campaign against the Persians. Ammianus' physical description of him (XXV, 4.22) is as follows. He was of medium stature. His hair lay flat on his head as if combed, his beard was shaggy and trimmed so as to end in a point. His eyes were clear and full of fire, an indication of the acuteness of his mind. His eyebrows were handsome, his nose very straight, and his mouth somewhat large with a pendulous lower lip. His neck was thick and somewhat bent, his shoulders large and broad. Moreover, from top to toe he bore a straight, well-proportioned bodily frame and as a result was strong and a good runner.

What of Julian as a general? Although he had had little practical experience of

Julian, dating from the 4th century AD or the early medieval period. He sports late Roman scale armour (*squama*) with detachable shoulder-guards, decorated with a lion's head. This statue, which was once though to be a 13th-century work from the time of Frederick II of Swabia, is considered to be one of the most true to life portraits of the apostate emperor. (Museo Diocesano di Acerenza, Italy; authors' photo, courtesy of the museum)

military matters, Ammianus tells us (XVI, 5.9) that he taught himself military tactics through the study of certain books, and so he would likely have been aware of much of Roman martial knowledge. Ammianus, writing after Julian's death, adds that he had a great fortitude in military matters, shown by the large number of battles he fought and by his conduct of wars, as well as by his ability to endure extreme cold and heat and his ability in the fight, being unafraid to engage himself directly on the battlefield. There are many notable examples of him demonstrating his knowledge of military matters: the sieges of cities and fortresses, undertaken amid the most extreme dangers, the varied forms in which he arranged his battle lines, the choice of safe and salubrious places to camp, and the wisely planned posting of frontier guards and field pickets.

Additionally, Julian had beside him a talented and experienced Magister Equitum in the person of **Severus**. We do not know much about him: he was an experienced and able commander who was dispatched to Gaul by the emperor to replace the dismissed Magister Equitum Marcellus. He immediately struck up a bond with the young *caesar*. Ammianus calls him

'a man neither subordinate nor overbearing but well known for his long and excellent record in the army'. He was of course one of the proponents of the idea of attacking the Alemanni at Argentoratum (Strasbourg), where he skilfully executed Julian's orders commanding the left wing of the army, avoiding the trap prepared by Serapio. He remained Julian's closest collaborator until the unexpected moment in which, during the campaign against Suomarius, after two years of campaigning alongside Julian, Severus showed a surprising timidity and hesitated to move deeper inside the enemy's territory. According to Ammianus, who labelled him a coward, Severus feared his own death, which resulted shortly afterwards, perhaps as a result of post-traumatic stress disorder or a nervous breakdown. We should remember that, at the time of Julian's campaign against Suomarius, Severus had valid reasons for urging caution to the emperor, who was forcing his poorly supplied, poorly paid and restless army deep into enemy territory.

A third key figure recorded in the campaign is the Frankish Tribune of the Cornuti **Bainobaudes**, who lost his life on the battlefield at Argentoratum. In AD 357, he was in Gaul, under the command of Julian. During the campaign, he distinguished himself in the seizing of several islands from the Alemanni. Lightly armed auxiliaries under his command swam across the Rhine, carrying their shields, and reached an island where the enemy believed themselves to be safe, and massacred them. They then re-entered the river and swam to another island, where they repeated their actions, until finally, tired of killing, they returned loaded with loot.

Details of the *humeralia* (shoulder-guards) of Julian's armour, on the Acerenza bust. This is the only example from late antiquity on which the *humeralia* are decorated with embossed figures, probably lions. This indicates that the shoulder-guards were made of metal as part of the original armour. (Museo Diocesano di Acerenza, Italy; authors' photo, courtesy of the museum)

GERMANIC

Ammianus (XVI, 12.4) states that **Chnodomar** was a man who caused 'universal turmoil and confusion', but outside the context of Julian's campaign, we find little significant mention of him. Of considerable height and strength, he was nicknamed *Gigas* ('Giant') by the Romans (Libanius, 143).

In AD 350, he was encouraged by the Roman emperor Constantius II, who was engaged in the East against the Sassanids, to attack Roman Gaul in order to engage the usurper Magnentius, who had turned against Constantius' brother the emperor Constans I and killed him. The Alemannic kings entered Roman territory and defeated the Roman army commanded by Decentius, brother of Magnentius and his *caesar*: after this victory, Chnodomar was able to freely loot Gaul.

In the AD 357 campaign, Chnodomar succeeded in inflicting a resounding defeat on Barbatio, who retired to winter quarters prematurely, leaving Julian alone against a superior force. Chnodomar decided to challenge Julian in the open field outside Argentoratum (Strasbourg).

A mature Germanic warrior, one of the herms found at Welschbillig Castle, Germany. Some of the Welschbillig herms are yet to be identified, but may represent prominent Germanic leaders of the Late Roman period who were probably Roman allies, like Charietto or, following Julian's victory at Argentoratum, Suomarius and Hortarius. Chnodomar's appearance would likely have been similar to this. (Rheinisches Landesmuseum Trier; author's photo, courtesy of the museum)

The right wing of the Alemannic army at Argentoratum was entrusted to **Serapio**, Chnodomar's nephew, who was 'still a young man with downy cheeks', and whose name, Ammianus informs us, would have been Agenarichus if his father Mederichus had not initiated him into certain Greek mysteries. Ammianus also informs us that the barbarian army, which was partly formed from mercenaries and partly from warriors under the command of their rulers, contained five kings (*reges* – **Vestralpus**, **Urius**, **Ursicinus**, **Suomarius** and **Hortarius**), ten regional princes (*regales*) and a long train of nobles (*optimates*).

With the exception of Serapio, the other kings were treated like lieutenants in Chnodomar's army and were subordinate to him. We know virtually nothing about them, save the fact that they were compelled by their own men to dismount before the battle because the barbarian infantry feared their leaders would abandon them when faced with defeat. This is a clear sign of the lack of confidence the Alemannic warriors had in their leaders. Two of them, Suomarius and Hortarius, fled the battlefield, according to both Ammianus and Zosimus.

OPPOSING FORCES

ROMAN

The Roman military system in the age of Julian

The great reform of the Roman army at the end of the 3rd century and the beginning of the 4th century AD consisted of the division of troops into two separate armies. The first of these was located on the *limes* (frontier), and was made up of *ripenses* (later denominated as *limitanei*). The second, the *comitatenses*, formed mobile reserves, and soon came to be seen as elite troops. Constantine improved this division.

The *ripenses* defended the frontiers operating as border guards and garrisoning forts and towns, with the help of local troops placed in strongholds (*burgi*). They chiefly consisted of new-style units of *equites* (cavalry, sometimes reduced to *cunei* or 'wedges' on the Danubian frontier) and *auxilia* (auxiliaries), or the traditional *alae*, *legiones* and *cohortes*. These *ripenses* were grouped into armies covering one or more provinces, under the command of a *dux* ('leader'). In Africa only, the frontier was under the control of the Praepositi Limitis under the supervision of a *comes*, the commander of a powerful mobile army.

The *comitatenses* (from the Latin *comitatus*, meaning armed escort or retinue) were positioned deeper within Roman territory, in order to defend it against barbarian raids. They were not garrisoned in fixed locations like the *limitanei*. Unless they were campaigning, they were stationed in towns, in which they had the right to occupy one-third of the available accommodation. They were composed of *legiones* of regular troops from the mobile army, of Legiones Palatinae and of Auxilia Palatina (elite troops).

The Auxilia Palatina, which were often formed of barbarians who joined the Roman army, were first raised by Constantine (perhaps to strengthen one of Maximianus'

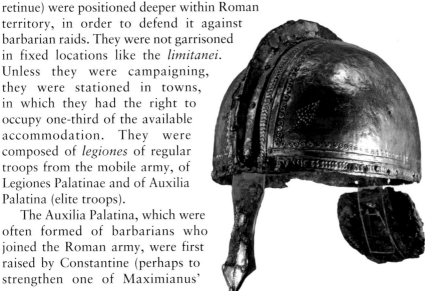

Late Roman ridge helmet found at Augsburg-Pfersee, end of the second quarter of the 4th century AD. Such specimens were reserved for officers. The helmet is made of iron, covered in gilded silver 0.1–0.3mm thick, and its bowl is 24cm long and 14.8cm high. Like most helmets of this type, it is formed from two iron halves, joined at the metallic crest. Between the iron parts and the silver covering was a black substance (probably pitch or resin), which also filled the indentations of the raised decorations. The iron crest is *c*.1mm thick, is 2.2cm high at its peak and extends at the front and the rear by about 8mm. The nose-guard is directly attached to the bowl; two conical nails are still visible on it, and the remaining section measures 8.3 x 2.7 x 0.6cm. The cheek-guards were fastened to the bowl with leather laces, as was the neck protector. The interior of the helmet was lined with leather. (Germanisches Nationalmuseum Nürnberg; authors' photo, courtesy of the museum)

Ridge helmet of the Deurne-Berkasovo type (variant 2a), 4th century AD. The importance of this helmet, found in the Balkans, lies in the curved brow, which is identical to the ridge helmets shown on the Arch of Constantine. Traces of gilding are present. The bowl, as in all helmets of this type, is divided in two with two parallel horizontal ribs. The ridge-crest is undecorated and is slightly raised. Note the wide cheek-guards (measuring 13.4cm x 8.3cm), which match the helmets on the frieze on the Arch of Constantine. The strong, compact neck-guard featuring two pairs of slots and angled collar appears to suggest a corded fastening system. (Private collection, photo courtesy of the owner)

reforms). They constituted the shock troops of the Roman army and came to the fore during Julian's campaigning. The longest established were the Cornuti ('horned men', recruited from a Germanic tribe bearing the same name, depicted on the Arch of Constantine with helmets bearing two small horns on the front), and the Bracchiati ('armlet wearers'), Iovii and the Victores.

The later document known as *Notitia Dignitatum* lists most of the infantry and cavalry units mentioned by the sources at the Battle of Argentoratum or that formed part of the *comitatus* of Julian in Gaul: the Batavi, Reges, Heruli, Petulantes, Celtae Moesiaci, Pannoniciani and Dalmati. Some of these names provide clear evidence of the degree of barbarization of the Roman army. These elite Germanic troops were recruited through levies on the tribes of the Upper Rhine and the *laeti* of Gaul. Sometimes, whole tribes were incorporated as auxiliaries. Other single tribes joined up by offering their arms to the Romans, as did groups of Franks, Alemanni and Vandals. These

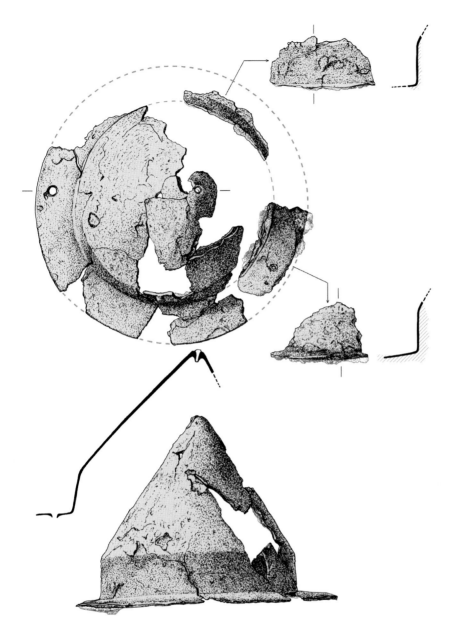

Fragmentary late Roman *umbo* (boss) from Koblenz, Florinsmarkt, grave no. 1, second half of 4th century AD. The recently discovered Koblenz finds include fragments of 12 helmets and three conical shield bosses in iron. The latter belong to the pointed Rhenen-Vermand type, widely diffused in the age of Julian. Although originally introduced into the Roman army by Germans, by this date they formed an integral part of Roman weaponry. (Dr Christian Miks)

warriors fought in the Palatine legions side by side with Roman soldiers. Very often these Germans – as well as provincial citizens of Numidian or Celtic ethnic origins – achieved great success in their military careers and some of them went on to hold high command.

The chain of command created by Constantine was composed of the emperor (*augustus*) who acted as supreme commander of the army, the *caesar* as deputy commander, and, beneath them two high-ranking officers, the infantry commander (Magister Peditum) and the cavalry commander (Magister Equitum). The former commanded the infantry forces of his assigned praetorian prefecture. The Praetorianus Praefectus, whose military functions these two new offices absorbed, was still responsible for the logistics and supply of the army. It was impossible to place all the mobile army under the immediate command of the emperor, so regional armies

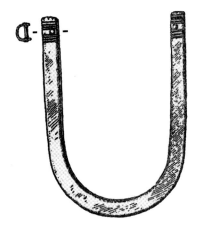

(such as those of Gaul, Illyricum, the Danube and the East) were instituted, commanded by a Magister Equitum on behalf of the emperor. When Julian died in AD 363, his successor inherited an army comprising some 150 units.

The organization of the Late Roman army in Gaul

Diocletian and Constantine had reinforced the administrative system throughout all the provinces of the empire, but had separated out its civil and military strands. The territory of Gaul was divided into further provinces, shared among two dioceses (*diocesis*): Gaul, with eight *provinciae* and Augusta Treverorum (Trier) as capital, and Julia Viennensis, composed of seven *provinciae* with Vienna (Vienne) as its principal city. The ancient province of Lugdunensis was divided into four provinces (from the rule of Constantine onwards). The residence of the Praefectus Praetorii Galliarum was in Augusta Treverorum (Trier), near the imperial palace.

The Gallic *comitatenses* would act when ordered to do so, garrisoned in cities or in temporary *castra* (fortified camps) while *limitanei* and Germanic *laeti* guarded the borders. Here, special areas were trusted to territorial commanders (*duces*). It is difficult to say if the duchies mentioned in the *Notitia Dignitatum* for Gaul (AD 385) already existed at the time of Julian. The Dux Maxima Sequanorum, which connected the south of Germania Prima to the cities of the Helvetians and Raurici, certainly did exist. It defended the Upper Rhine, from Lake Constance to Horbourg. The *Notitia Dignitatum* (oc., XLII) continues to refer to a *provincia* (province) of Gallia Riparensis, commanded by a Dux Galliae Riparensis. The army created by Diocletian was camped on the Rhine and Lac Léman. Simple *cohortes* defended Marseille and the Savoie. The *dux* also covered the area north and east of the Rhône, guarding the Alps and Rhône river routes. The presence of a Dux Raetiae and of a Dux Germaniae Primae, after AD 290 and until the time of the *Notitia Dignitatum*, also affected the location of troops pertinent to the ancient legions in Argentoratum. The Dux Belgicae Primae was based in Augusta Treverorum (Trier). From the mid-4th century AD the north-western coastal region required more attention than previously, and so a Comes Maritimi Tractus assumed responsibility for Armorica.

Substantially three commands, one per province, shared the defence of the Rhine area. They were based in Vesontio (Besançon), Mogontiacum (Mainz) and Colonia Agrippinensis (Cologne). To them was added the Dux Belgicae Secundae, responsible for the defence of the Atlantic coast. Other military forces – comprising the *comitatenses* field army, the fluvial fleets, the *laeti* and the Sarmatians, who were also stationed inside the territory – remained under the direct command of the Magister Militum intra Gallias.

Diocletian doubled the number of legions, but the number of troops within each was lower than before, each legion containing barely more than 1,000 men, even though the historical name of the legion was maintained. Many of the new legions were in fact independent *vexillationes* (detachments) from the old ones. Ammianus mentions mobile detachments that were 300 or 500 strong. Most of them were turned into *limitanei* and troop detachments from them went to serve abroad. The army of the *limes* did not benefit from any increase in manpower: the *comitatenses* would be dispatched to the border areas in case of enemy attack and would remain there until the situation was restored. As a result of the depopulation of north-eastern Gaul, which began in the 3rd century AD, these provinces had gradually become a military border zone between the Roman Empire and the barbarian territories. From this point onwards, some of the occupants of the devastated areas were no longer simple defenceless peasants or slaves of landowners, but Germanic or Sarmatian colonists and soldiers settled by the will of the emperors in Gaul. On the one hand, they constituted a reservoir of forces for offensive operations for the mobile army, but also provided armed territorial defensive groups immediately available to counter unannounced threats. Thanks to their mastery of warfare, the auxiliaries of the Late Empire were no longer mere auxiliary troops as in previous centuries, but formed elite units of the Roman army.

A reconstruction by Dr Christian Miks of one of the helmets found at Koblenz (grave 1). It presents an idealized version of a Deurne-Berkasovo type (variant 2a) ridge helmet. This type of helmet was made of two half-bowls joined at an intersecting ridge crest, and fitted with rounded ear-guards and a nose-guard. (Andrei Negin)

Constantine dispersed the *comitatenses* around Gaul until the middle of the 4th century AD. According to our available sources, the disposition of legionary troops in Gaul after the death of Constantine was as follows:

1. Armorica, in Gallia Lugdunensis III, was defended by Legio I Flavia Martis or Metis and Legio I Flavia Pacis (then part of Julian's mobile army), together with local *limitanei*, the Benetis (naval troops) or Namnetes, against the incursions of Franks and Saxons.

2. The Ioviani operated in the area of Augusta Treverorum (Trier) and Arelate (Arles), probably together with the Herculiani (Legio II Herculia).

3. The Legio I Martia or Martiorum Victrix was located in the *provincia* of Maxima Sequanorum or Sequania, at Augusta Rauracorum (Augst) and in the Castrum Rauracensis.

To these units we should also add the Moesiaci, the Menapii, the Armigeri Defensores and the Ballistarii Dafnenses. The latter were stationed in Augustodunum (Autun) in Gallia Lugdunensis I, where a *fabrica* (workshop) for manufacturing *ballistae* (crossbow engines) was located (*Notitia Dignitatum*, oc., IX, 33, 34).

As far as the cavalry is concerned, in the 3rd century AD the presence in Samarobriva (Amiens) of a Numerus Catafractariorum is mentioned, and is referred to again there around AD 380 (*Equites Catafractarii Ambianenses*, *Notitia Dignitatum*, oc., VI, 36).

Gaul was deprived of its main mobile army during Magnentius' uprising. Without this, Gaul was not able to counter the threat of Germanic invasion, and the Gallic garrisons along the border collapsed in about AD 350. At this point, the invasions deprived the empire of half of its military strength and ruined Constantine's efforts.

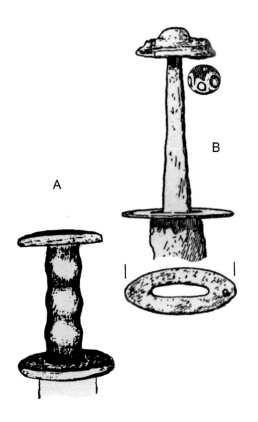

Tactics

Although it seems incongruous, before Julian's arrival in Gaul the preferred tactic used by Late Roman emperors against an invasion was, having gained some minor victories in several indecisive clashes, to reach an agreement with the invaders, and settle them inside or outside the borders as military colonists. This idea was first and foremost an initial response to the complexity of irregular warfare in north-eastern Gaul. Conversely, the incorporation of Barbarians allowed the establishment of a territorial defence in depth along the borders. In addition, these foreign recruits brought about adaptations in tactics, allowing Roman forces to fight more effectively by using non-conventional military methods.

The search for surprise and indirect approaches also led the Romans to use counter-offensive tactics that further destabilized the situation. In July AD 356, in order to counter the Alemannic raiding parties infesting the region between Augustobona (Troyes) and Augustodunum (Autun), Julian decided to conduct a raid with 300 horsemen through hostile territory accompanied by a troop of 8,000 Roman auxiliaries: 'And to avoid any delay, he took only the Catafractarii and the Ballistarii, who were far from suitable to defend a general, and traversing the same road, he came to Autessiodurum [Auxerre]' (Ammianus XVI, 2.3–5).

Roman sword hilts, dating from the second half of the 4th century AD. A: hilt of a sword from Wiesbaden-Mainz-Kostheim, with upper iron rivet showing traces of niello, and an iron pommel and guard. B: hilt of a sword from Nydam, with a horn pommel, conical hilt, and guard made of horn. (Andrea Salimbeti, after Miks)

Julian surprised his opponents, harassed them continuously with his armoured cavalry, which was normally employed in frontal attacks in pitched battles (Nazarius, *Panegyricus Constantino Augusto dictus*, *Panegyrici Latini*, X, 23.4). He employed extreme mobility against the Barbarians, which the Sarmatians and Alans executed perfectly. Such tactics were far removed from the more predictable movements of conventional forces. A few weeks later, Julian left Durocorturum (Reims) with his entire army and resumed conventional methods by attacking 'in close columns the bands of Alemanni' in the region around Decem Pagi (Dieuze). However, as Ammianus records:

> because the day was misty and overcast, so that even objects close at hand could not be seen, the enemy, aided by their acquaintance with the country, went around by way of a crossroad and made an attack on the two legions bringing up the rear of the Caesar's army. And they would nearly have annihilated them, had not the shouts that they suddenly raised brought up the reinforcements of our allies. Then and thereafter, thinking that he could cross neither roads nor rivers without any ambushes, Julian was wary and hesitant, which is a special merit in great commanders, and is wont both to help and save their armies. (Ammianus, XVI, 2.9–11)

Because of the irregular methods employed by the Germanic warriors, doubts gradually crept into the normally efficient Roman minds about how best to confront them, and for this reason the Romans incorporated specialist irregular troops in combat. In AD 358, around Augusta Treverorum (Trier), the Chamavi were not confident enough to launch a major campaign against the Romans, but 'were intent on secret excursions, and plunder, by which they did great damage to the country'. The barbarians outmanoeuvred the Romans tactically in this respect: 'Caesar, was at this time unable to restrain the nocturnal and clandestine incursions of the Barbarians, as they robbed in small parties, straggling from each other, and when day appeared, not one of them was visible'. Julian therefore accepted the services of Charietto, an irregular Frankish warrior who had chosen to fight for the empire. His irregular methods included night-time infiltration by small groups into wooded areas under Chamavi control, terror and intimidation raids, and the systematic decapitation of any captured enemy warriors. Charietto's methods were highly effective, and Julian added 'to them many of the Salii, against the plundering Chamavi, who though they lived on what they stole, yet were probably less expert in the art of robbing, than these men who had studied it. In the day he guarded the open fields, and killed all that escaped his robbers' (Zosimus, III, 6.4; III, 7.1–7).

Late Roman helmet of the Dunapentele-Intercisa type from Worms, Germany, dating from the second half of the 4th century AD. This light helmet was probably used by the infantry, rather than the cavalry. However, recent finds at Koblenz indicate that silver-coated helmets were not only the preserve of officers or elite troops, but were also worn by the *comitatenses* mobile troops and regular *limitanei* soldiers. (Dr Christian Miks)

One basic function fulfilled by soldiers of foreign origin was the acquisition of intelligence, an essential function that allowed the Roman columns to strike back at an irregular opponent using evasive tactics. To obtain such information, Julian encouraged defectors from the enemy to serve in his army. In AD 359, the tribune Hariobaud, who was of Alemannic origin, was sent by Julian on an intelligence-gathering mission against his own people; his ability to speak the language of the barbarians and the ease with which he could easily reach the border area would facilitate his monitoring of the enemy's movements. Furthermore, raiding operations using barbarian auxiliaries were also launched by Julian, for instance in order to seize scouts or sources of useful information in barbarian-occupied territory. In AD 358, when preparing an expedition against the Alemannic king Hortarius, Julian ordered two officers of Germanic origin to infiltrate enemy territory in order to 'capture a prisoner at any cost' (Ammianus, XVII, 10.3).

In open battle, the tactics employed against the barbarians were adapted to the circumstances. Ammianus confirms that the Roman army of the 4th century AD had retained its earlier tactical capacities. At the Battle of Brocomagus (Brumath) in AD 356, Julian disposed his troops in a two-pronged formation (*bicornis figura*) against the Alemanni. As the two sides met, the barbarians were pressed on all sides and yielded. Ammianus' description clearly records the use of a pincer manoeuvre (*forfex*). The *bicornis figura* effectively possess two flanks: external (formed by the two wings of the attacking force), and the interior (formed by the division of the force into two pincer elements, along the central axis).

At Argentoratum, Julian directed the battle from the centre to the rear. When his elite armoured cavalry, in which he placed much hope, was driven away in panic, the *caesar* was able to respond to defeat of the Roman cavalry on the right by using his infantry in the centre. On the Roman left, Severus carried out his orders to protect the army's left flank effectively. The use of compact shield-wall formations (*scutorum conpagis*), held in *modo testudinis* (tortoise shell), probably provided the fulcrum for the Roman effort.

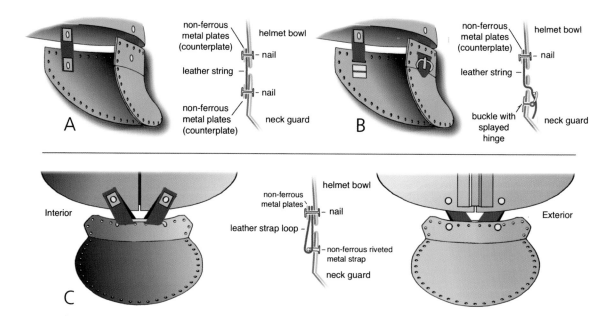

A

B

Interior

C

Exterior

non-ferrous metal plates (counterplate)
helmet bowl
– nail
leather string –
– nail
non-ferrous metal plates (counterplate)
neck guard

non-ferrous metal plates (counterplate)
helmet bowl
– nail
leather string –
buckle with splayed hinge
neck guard

helmet bowl
non-ferrous metal plates
– nail
leather strap loop –
– non-ferrous riveted metal strap
neck guard

Diagrams showing how Late Roman neck-guards were fastened, in two different variants. (Dr Christian Miks)

Weaponry

On the Arch of Constantine, a particular type of pseudo-Attic helmet is shown being worn by the Auxilia Palatina infantrymen of the Cornuti, furnished with wide cheek-guards and a large neck-guard. These specimens, as they are represented in the figurative sources, show a widening towards the rear, offering more protection to the neck. This type of helmet is visible on the head of Eastern legionaries and officers from the 3rd century AD onwards, as depicted on monuments at Dura Europos and Palmyra, as well as on Western figurative monuments of the Tetrarchy and the early rule of Constantine, such as the group of sculptures at Langres.

The helmets on the Arch of Constantine are decorated with a pair of winged horns attached to the frontal Attic diadem. These 'horns' were made of metal and were added to represent the symbol of the unit, the *cornua*, which referred to its Teutonic origin. The horns, instead of being laterally disposed, emerge from the centre of the rim above the forehead of the warrior; Alfoldi and Ross have suggested that they are goat horns. On the arch, the horns are also depicted on top of ridge helmets of Sassanian origin, demonstrating not only the precision of the artist, but also how the equipment varied among troops of the same unit. Forked plumes are also represented on the helmets worn by other marching soldiers on the arch, with less pronounced neck-guards, again representing the Auxilia Palatina of the Cornuti.

From the end of the 3rd and throughout all of the 4th and 5th centuries AD, the ridge helmet was one of the most common types employed by the Late Roman legionary and *auxilia*. In Julian's time, such helmets are shown in various works of art, such as those found in the Catacombs of Syracusa in Sicily, and the mosaics of Villa Romana del Tellaro, both in Sicily. They feature a metallic crest similar to the lighter Intercisa type, or the heavier type used by generals and emperors, gilded and decorated with peacock feathers. Some fine surviving examples probably dating to the time of Julian and Constantius include the following:

1. The 12 fragmentary examples from the Koblenz find.
2. Two to four examples found at the Iatrus Fortress, at Krivina, Bulgaria.
3. The two magnificent specimens covered with gilded silver from Augsburg-Pfersee (Augusta Vindelicorum).
4. An example from Trier (Augusta Treverorum).
5. The example from Burgh Castle, whose *terminus post quem* is AD 336/341.
6. The example from Telița, Romania.
7. The fragmentary remains of a helmet from Singidunum (Belgrade).
8. The finds from Keszthely-Fenékpuszta, Hungary dated to AD 351–54.

Roman infantry and cavalry also wore conical segmented helmets, originally based on oriental models, and composed of four to six radial bands (spangenhelm). Beneath the helmet, soldiers wore a helmet lining (*cento*, Ammianus, XIX, 8.8) and the pillbox hat known as the *pileus pannonicus*, which can be seen on many monuments such as the Roman garrison soldiers in the Via Latina catacombs in Rome.

Julian's helmet as emperor can be seen on his coins and it conforms to the heavy ridge helmet type, exemplified by the well-known Berkasovo and Budapest forms. The helmets on his coins relate to the period in which Julian was already *Augustus*, but, apart from the imperial diadem, they show an identical shape to the one worn by Achilles, who is dressed in military imperial accoutrement, in the Villa Romana del Tellaro mosaic. This ridge-type helmet is a simple gilded version divided in two by a central join and topped with a plume of peacock feathers.

The traditional *lorica segmentata* seems to have survived in this period only within some Spanish legions, while most parts of infantry armour were made of mail (like the *lorica* of the *centenarius* represented on the Hypogeum of Via Dino Compagni, Rome), iron and bronze scales (*squama*). The muscled armour in metal or leather (*thorakion heroikon*), which is only (but clearly) referred to in iconography, with the exception of a possible specimen in bronze from the Axel Guttmann collection, seems to have been worn by emperors, officers, members of the guard and elite troops.

Many Roman soldiers fought without armour, bearing only their clothing, helmet, shield and offensive weapons. The latter consisted of the *spatha* (long sword), the (shorter) *semispatha*, javelin (such as the *verutta*) and darts (*plumbatae* or *martiobarbuli*, which could be stored on the interior face of the shield). Barbed javelins like the Germanic *angon* were also used. The spear, which tended to replace the *pila* and other javelins in face-to-face combat, was often painted with alternating colours.

Helmets were sometimes not even worn, especially by the barbarian auxiliaries. Shields (*scuta*) were mostly oval or round in shape, decorated on the exterior face by the *episemata* or *deigmata* of the unit, allowing recognition by friend and foe.

Late Roman *spatha* (straight sword) from Ildesheim, last quarter of the 4th century AD. The sword is 85cm long. Note its bronze pommel, the remains of the wooden grip and gilded scabbard mouth. (Rheinisches Landesmuseum Trier; author's photo, courtesy of the museum)

Reconstructions of Roman *milites* (soldiers) of the Legio Palatina of the Primani and the Auxilia Palatina of the Celtae, at the time of the Battle of Argentoratum. (Reconstruction by Igor Dzis and Raffaele D'Amato)

The dress of some Roman soldiers from the time of Julian is well illustrated in many monuments, like the splendid mosaics at the Villa Romana del Tellaro. Here, a great hunting scene shows *milites* (infantry) and *equites* (cavalry) from around AD 350–60 dressed in off-white *tunicae* (tunics), indicating they are probably *palatini*. These tunics are decorated with purple *segmenta*, *loroi*, and *orbiculi* (bands). The *paludamenta/Chlamydes* (cape) of high-ranking officers, fastened on the right side by crossbow *fibulae* (brooches), were reddish-brown in colour.

The size of the Roman force at Argentoratum

Ammianus, our primary source for details of Julian's Gallic campaign, tells us that Roman forces were significantly outnumbered going into battle. There seems to be, among historians, a general consensus about the size of the Roman army, in line with Ammianus' figure of around 13,000 troops. Drinkwater estimates the size to have been between 13,000 and 15,000 soldiers. We should remember that Ammianus was involved in the organizational administration of the army, and had access to troop records.

It is also important to consider the quality and the composition of the Roman army: in terms of discipline, armament, organization and strategy, Julian's army was far superior to his barbarian counterpart's. In addition to the 360 guardsmen that accompanied the *caesar* to Gaul (Equites Scutarii and Equites Gentiles, Ammianus, XVI, 4.1–12), Julian's army was composed of a number of experienced auxiliary units accustomed to fighting alongside each other. They were the feared Auxilia Palatina of Germanic and Celtic origin, the Celtae, the Petulantes (Ammianus, XX, 4.2), the Cornuti, the Bracchiati, the Reges (i.e. the Regii Auxilium Palatinum), the Heruli and the Batavi. The Batavi were not a single unit of cavalry, because they are mentioned by Ammianus together with the other *auxilia*, the Regii, Batavi and Regibus, and there is no mention of action from a reserve cavalry unit. These *auxilia* units (each about 500 strong) were particularly effective against the Alemanni when paired with the heavily armed and armoured Roman legionaries. The Regii, however, provide a point of debate, over whether they were an Auxilia Palatina, or a Legio Palatina (the Regii Emeseni Iudaei) transferred to Gaul in February AD 356 from Alexandria. Zuckerman's interpretation, that this unit fought as a rear-guard and not in the front line as was usual for the legions, supports the theory that they were *auxilia*.

Among the legions (numbering between 500 and 1,000 men) the place of honour was given to the Primani. The Primani (Ammianus, XVI, 12.49) were a Legio Palatina that Constantine had already integrated into the mobile army. The origins of the Primani are difficult to identify with precision; according to some authors, it came from a *vexillatio* of the old Legio I Italica, according to others from a *vexillatio* of Legio I Julia, while others still consider it to have come from one of the new Legio I Flavia Pacis or the Legio I Flavia Gallicana Constantia. Considering that the latter is mentioned by name in the *Notitia Dignitatum*, the first or second hypothesis is the most likely.

Ammianus, who served on the military staff in this period and was also in Gaul under Julian until leaving his service shortly before the battle, also mentions the Moesiaci (XX, 1.3), while the Ioviani (Legio I Iovia) and the Herculiani, although not mentioned in the sources, were already in the Comitatus of Magnentius, and were therefore inherited by Julian. Hoffmann also suggests the presence of the Armigeri Defensores and the Martenses in Julian's army in the campaign of AD 356–60, and of the Legio I Flavia Pacis. Units of the Legio I Martia were also present; their camp was attacked by the Alemanni in AD 354, and the survivors incorporated into Julian's army. The army also featured men of the Ballistarii Dafnenses, who (according to Ammianus, XVI, 2.5) escorted the *caesar* from Vienna (Vienne) to Autessiodurum (Auxerre) alongside the Clibanarii. Solari also proposes the presence of the Tungrecani legion, possibly identifying with the auxiliaries (not the Auxilia Palatina) under the command of Severus.

The cavalry was composed of *vexillationes* of the Equites Sagittarii (horse archers, feared by the Germans, Ammianus, XVI, 12.7), the Clibanarii and the Equites Catafractarii (two *vexillationes*, XVI, 12.63), and probably also of the light Equites Dalmati (possibly three elite *vexillationes*) who had already been integrated into the Comitatus of Magnentius. In total, Julian's force comprised five legions, detachments from perhaps five other legions, seven Auxilia Palatina and other auxiliary units, and seven cavalry units.

The *stela* (stone slab) of a Signifer of Limitanei called Lepontius, from the mid-4th century AD; this is a cast from the lost original, in Strasbourg Archaeological Museum. Precise dating of this *stela* is very difficult, but it is one of the few from the 4th century AD to have survived. Lepontius may have served under Julian during his campaign against the Alemanni. His helmet is difficult to identify precisely, and may be of a simple Dunapentele-Intercisa type, or a conical spangenhelm, fitted with a horse's tail (*juba equina*). He is armed with *hasta* (spear), *spatha* (sword) and round *scutum* (shield), and noteworthy is his *sagum* (cloak) fastened on the right shoulder by a crossbow *fibula* (brooch). A cockerel is depicted on the standard next to his left shoulder. The inscription reads Lepontius (?) [---] All [---] // [-----]? (Jasper Oorthuys © Karwansaray Publishers)

The Signifer of Limitanei Lepontius was the standard bearer of a Ripenses unit, serving in the Rhine valley, along the Tractum Argentoratensis. His Celtic–Germanic appearance and the cockerel on his standard suggest he was part of a *laeti* unit. Valdemeri suggests that the presence of the cockerel may indicate he is a Heliodromus (Courier of the Sun), a high-ranking member of the Mithraic religion, or may even have Christian references. (Jasper Oorthuys © Karwansaray Publishers)

GERMANIC

The size of the Germanic force

The numbers, as always, are controversial and the subject of much debate among modern scholars. Warry and Goldsworthy consider Ammianus' figure of 35,000 warriors to be speculative; two authors are explicitly critical of Ammianus in this regard and offer their own estimates: Delbrück estimates between only 6,000 and 10,000 Alemanni to have been present, while Drinkwater proposes a figure of 15,000 men based on a core of 9,000, a 4,000-strong levy and 2,000 allies. The latter estimate is more recent, the author in question having more specifically researched this period and location, and is more consistent with the typically meticulous Roman body count of 6,000–8,000 Alemanni. Wucherpfennig also criticizes the figure given by Ammianus.

Against these scholarly opinions, Hugh Elton and Duncan Head argue on behalf of Ammianus, accepting his figure of 35,000 *armati* (soldiers), taking into account the presence of non-combatants and servants according to mid-4th century AD Alemannic social norms. Incidentally, both Elton and Drinkwater accept that only 20–25 per cent of the barbarians present comprised fighting warriors. Considering the number of Alemannic leaders present, at least 17 senior figures and their retinues entered the fight, which means that each of them was at the head of 2,000 men, providing a total of 34,000 warriors. If we consider that the nobles (*optimates*) could also command small retinues, we can add an extra 1,000 or so men. It is also important to bear in mind the following information: Julian personally surrounded himself with a retinue of 200 *scholarii* (Ammianus, XVI, 12.28). Chnodomar was in the company of 200 warriors when he was captured after the Battle of Argentoratum (Ammianus, XVI, 12.60).

Libanius, who was close to Julian and who penned his funeral oration, affirms that the *caesar* gave battle at the moment when the Germanic warriors crossing the Rhine River were not so few as to make any victory useless, but not so many as to make it impossible. Thus, despite the criticisms of exaggeration by Roman writers, it is possible that Roman troops were superior in number to the Germanic ones at the time of the Argentoratum clash. It can also be argued that 35,000 men comprised the total force available to the Alemanni, but not necessarily the figure that took part in the battle.

The relinquished weapons of defeated warriors under various leaders found in Denmark can help us extrapolate how many warriors may have been attached to a Germanic leader. For example, the finds at Ejsbed (dating to around AD 300) indicate that the defeated force comprised about 200 warriors, including nine horsemen and 60 warriors armed with swords. The defeated Germanic armies found here had a size varying between 200 and 600 men, which equates to the figures for each war band according to Ammianus.

Historians estimate the total population of 'Alemannia' to have been around 120,000–150,000 people at this point, a very small figure in relation

to the approximately 10 million who inhabited Gaul. This numerical discrepancy was counterbalanced by the fact that Alemannic society, vexed by the continuous struggles between the various clans that composed it, constituted a rich source of military manpower: it is estimated that in total the Alemanni were able to mobilize up to 30,000–40,000 warriors.

Alemannic military organization

The Alemannic confederation originated in the Main Valley in central Germany, and then moved to the Agri Decumates (roughly corresponding to the modern state of Baden-Württemberg in south-western Germany), a region that had been part of Germania Superior for 150 years until abandoned by the Romans in the 3rd century AD. Here, on the eastern bank of the Rhine, the Alemanni founded a series of communities known as *pagi*, of uncertain number, which probably changed over time. Normally combined in pairs, *pagi* could join to form kingdoms (*regna*), on a probably permanent and hereditary basis. According to Ammianus, the Alemannic rulers are described in various terms: *reges excelsiores ante alios* ('kings excelling over other kings'), *reges proximi* ('local kings'), *reguli* ('lesser kings') and *regales* ('princes'). Perhaps this formed a formal hierarchy, or perhaps they merely represent overlapping definitions in the sources. It seems that in AD 357, just prior to the Battle of Argentoratum, there were two *reges excelsiores* (Chnodomar and Vestralpus), who perhaps acted as 'first among equals' within the confederation, and a further five or six *reges* (Ammianus, XVI, 12.1), considering that the territories of the confederation stretched along the Rhine. It is possible that the so-called *reguli* were the rulers of one of the two *pagi* that formed a *regnum*. Regarding social organization, below the royal family there were the nobles (*optimates*) and the warriors (*armati*), the latter divided into the class of professional warriors and the free men's levy. Each nobleman was able to gather about 50 warriors.

The sites that have been excavated and researched on the edge of the Black Forest, opposite the Late Roman *limes* on the Rhine, give us an idea of how a Germanic invading army could have been structured and positioned, as well as the military aspects of a *pagus* settlement. On the hill at Offenburg, for example,

Shields of the Bucinobantes (Alemanni) listed in the different versions of the *Notitia Dignitatum*, under the command of the Magister Militum Praesentalis II. Ammianus relates (XXIX, 4.7) how a contingent of Bucinobantes under their king Macrianus was sent to Britain by Valentinian I, and how Macrianus was later killed while allied to Rome fighting the Franks (XXX, 3.7). Considering that the Eastern Part of the *Notitia* was compiled around AD 380, such devices could have been used by some Germanic warriors at the Battle of Argentoratum. (Andrea Salimbeti)

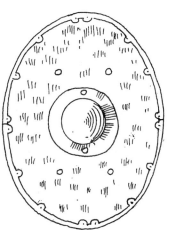
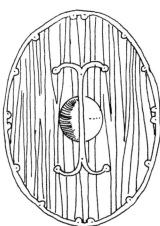

Reconstruction of a Germanic shield, from a grave at Mannheim-Feudenheim, Germany. (Andrea Salimbeti, after Schlette)

between 200 and 300 warriors were located, whereas on the Zähringen Castle hill near Freiburg, within an area of 3.5 ha, there were some 600–800 men temporarily stationed.

The transformation of these fortified hills into settlements occurred in the second half of the 4th century AD and at the beginning of the 5th century AD. Small warrior strongholds were transformed into residences of the Germanic or Alemannic elite, forming a prestigious location connected to the needs of military security. This becomes clear, for instance, from the excavations performed by German archaeologists at Urach, whose extensive and high-quality material finds have been comprehensively analyzed by Ursula Koch. The two heights of Geisskopf and Kügeleskopf near Offenburg at the entrance to the Kinzigtal are located in a strategically important position, because they dominate the road from the Rhine into the Black Forest. This explains why there were Roman fortifications on both sides of the river dating from earlier periods (at Zunsweier and Rammersweier). Excavations on both these heights have revealed metal finds such as iron weapons and tools as well as some magnificent bronze fittings for a Late Roman military belt.

The hilltop strongholds served as the princely seats of independent Germanic followers or petty *reguli* kings, as attested by the concentration of warriors, the monopolization of metal crafts and the manufacture of weapons and belts.

At Argentoratum the Alemannic army comprised a mixture of war bands from at least nine cantons, some of whom were serving as mercenaries and the rest in accordance with pacts of mutual assistance (Ammianus, XVI, 12.26). Their number varied from 200 to 2,000 men and they were similar in composition and size to the Roman Auxilia Palatina. It is also possible that many warriors who fought for Chnodomar on the day of battle had previously served in the Roman army.

Tactics

The Rhineland *limes* and its Gallo-Roman hinterland were not theatres in which a conventional war could be waged. Pitched battles and sieges, common in Mesopotamia against the Persian Sassanids or in the infighting between Romans, was inconceivable in north-east Gaul. The Germanic aggressor had long since adapted to the manoeuvring of the highly trained Roman infantry. The former executed a 'small war', equating to harassment, raiding, avoidance of combat, and rapidly broken-off engagements, rather than deadly direct clashes. The difficulty for the Romans was not in winning a pitched battle, but in compelling an adversary 'accustomed to avoiding war' (*Panegyricus Constantino Augusto dictus*, VII, 12.2) to engage in battle. The Germanic irregulars sought to avoid confrontation by employing small detachments operating simultaneously in several directions, thus making direct clashes very difficult to engineer.

The Frankish and Alemannic confederations also had no strategic or even tactical interest in destroying the Roman army. Their aims were more limited to operations of 'back-and-forth' raids for looting or attempts to settle below the *limes*. The barbarians therefore refused the open field of battle, being too risky for them, as the events of Argentoratum would demonstrate. Instead, they opted for tactics that could circumvent Roman superiority in the open field. Since the legions were built to create and resist frontal shock combat, the barbarians evaded this relative invulnerability by refusing pitched battles,

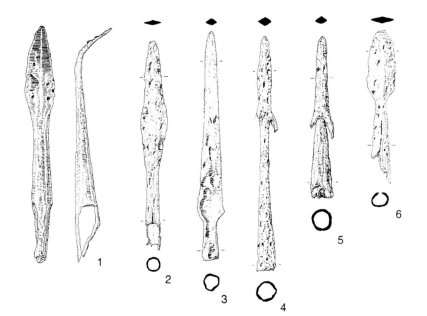

Alemannic shafted weapons, from a settlement near Offenburg. Nos. 1, 2, 3 and 6 are spear heads; nos. 4 and 5 are javelin heads of the *angon* type. Ammianus reports a large number of throwing weapons used by Germanic warriors during the Battle of Argentoratum: the *spicula* (a long javelin similar to the *pilum*, also known as an *angon*), *verruta* and *missilia* (short spears and javelins) and *ferratae arundines* (probably arrows and darts or the so-called '*franciscae*', typical Germanic throwing axes). (Andrea Salimbeti, after Steuer)

as well as by not performing long and strong sieges, and not allowing themselves to be besieged.

Similarly, on the defensive side, the Germanic tribes favoured harassment and ambushes, and chose difficult terrain for the Roman infantry and cavalry. From the opposing perspective, Ammianus' description of the Battle of Argentoratum shows how well the Germanic warriors were acquainted with Roman battle tactics and were also able to contemplate fighting a Roman army in a pitched battle. Roman writers point in particular to a Germanic battle tactic of closely grouped riders and infantrymen. Julius Caesar specifies that the latter were perfectly trained to fight with the former (*Gallic Wars*, I, 48). The infantry were quick to put themselves below the enemy's horses in order to slaughter them with their knives or daggers. Germanic horsemen were also more likely to dismount and fight on foot.

This is indeed what happened at Argentoratum, as indicated by the battle array of the Alemanni, who placed mixed, lightly armed infantry and their horsemen against the Roman cavalry during the battle. 'They realized that one of their warriors on horseback, no matter how skilful, in meeting one of our Clibanarii, must hold bridle and shield in one hand and brandish his spear in the other, and would thus be able to do no harm to a soldier protected by metal armour; whereas the infantry soldier in the hottest part of the fight, when nothing is apt to be guarded against except what is straight ahead of oneself, can move around low down and unseen, and by piercing a horse's side throw its unsuspecting rider headlong, whereupon he can be slain with little trouble' (Ammianus, XVI, 12.22).

Besides this, the main battle tactic was a frontal attack possibly in a wedge formation, seeking to pierce the enemy's battle array. The 'Germanic' origin of the wedge (*cuneus*), for those who had to defend against it, rests on the use of this word in ancient historiography to characterize the battle lines of the Western 'barbarian' populations from the 1st century AD. The armies of the Batavian leader Julian Civilis, in AD 69, employed this according to Tacitus (*Histories*, IV, 16.2; V, 15.1) at least twice.

Similarly, the initial disposition of the Alemanni at Argentoratum in AD 357 was a wedge, or rather, several wedges: 'When our leading officers spied them, now near at hand, taking their places in close wedge-formation, they halted and stood fast, making a solid line, like an impregnable wall, of the vanguard, the standard bearers, and the staff-officers; and with like wariness the enemy held their ground in wedge-formation' (Ammianus, XVI, 12.20). The *cuneus*, whether it was the equivalent of a Roman tactic or, in contrast, a purely Germanic disposition, seemed to be the preferred battle order of the Western 'barbarians'. Interestingly, in the late *sermo castrensis* (or vulgar Latin), the *cuneus romanus* was known informally as the *caput porcinum* (boar's head), which was very close to the Norse word *svinfylking* (boar's snout), designating a fighting tactic of the early Anglo-Saxon and Scandinavian Middle Ages.

However, the tactical formation known from ancient times by the name of *cuneus* existed well before the 'barbarization' of the Roman army, whatever date is attributed to it. It is attested to in the Roman army even before Tacitus, who was the first to use the word *cuneus* to designate the Germanic fighting formation. The lost *De Re Militari* of Cato (fragment 11), reported by Aulus Gellius (*Noctes Atticae*, X, 9.1) places it among the possible formations used by the Roman army the consular age. In 53 BC, the most experienced men in Quintus Cicero's troops in Atuatuca (Tongeren) formed a wedge to disengage themselves from an attack by Gallic Sugambri cavalrymen (*Gallic Wars*, VI, 40.2). Livy's *History* shows that the use of a wedge formation in training, stretching long back into Rome's history, was very common. For the historian Lammert, *svinfylking* does not correspond to the Latin *caput porci*, *fylking* simply having a very general meaning of 'battle order' and, probably, the present authors would like to add, corresponding to the Latin word *fulcum*. Lammert nevertheless retains the idea of a specific Germanic *cuneus*, proposing (alongside Gundel) specific wedge-formation training undertaken by Germanic warriors, although he struggles to determine exactly on which grounds it could be distinguished from the Roman one. The ancient literary sources are unfortunately not precise enough for us to fully understand the entire tactical technique of the Germanic wedge. It seems, however, that the western Germans, and before them the Celts, frequently adopted a relatively simple combat formation, consisting of a main line of infantry in dense order, presenting a wall of shields and spears to the enemy (Livy, *History*, X, 29.6–7 for the Celts; Dio Cassius, XXXVIII, 49). This fits perfectly with the weaponry employed by these populations, as well as with their lack of tactical division and their ability in collective movement. However, this tactical choice was more of a basic solution, which

Bust of a young Romanized Germanic warrior, probably a Roman bodyguard, from Welschbillig – a fine example of late provincial Roman art in Germany. The Rheinisches Landesmuseum contains 113 studies often representing warriors, such as this one, whose torques indicate he may have formed part of a Roman elite unit. His hairstyle and other aspects of his appearance were common to many Alemannic warriors. (Rheinisches Landesmuseum Trier; author's photo, courtesy of the museum)

might be set aside if the ground or the quality of the troops allowed more complex combat techniques to be employed. Presenting these Germanic tactics as a simple *cuneus* should not induce us to think that they consistently fought in dense order (see Livy, *History*, XL, 40.2–8, Caesar, *Gallic Wars*, VIII, 14.5, Tacitus, *Histories*, IV, 16.2, V, 16.1 and 18.1). Moreover, in some situations (and it is clear that at Argentoratum the Alemanni used wedge formations), the Germanic troops formed up in dense order and charged in a wedge. During the battle, by attacking the Roman lines in several wedge movements, they finally managed to break through the Roman ranks in one location, although they were then beaten back by the Roman reserves.

However, despite the evolutions noted, the tactical effectiveness of the Germanic armies in the Late Roman period remained inferior to that of the Roman forces. Ammianus notes during the Battle of Argentoratum that 'the Alemanni were stronger and taller, our soldiers disciplined by long practice; they were savage and uncontrollable, our men quiet and wary, these relying on their courage, while the Germans presumed upon their huge size' (XVI, 12.47).

Weaponry

The quality of the Germanic weapons uncovered had revealed additional information on the ranks within the Alemannic confederation. The elite warriors such as kings, princes, *optimates* and their retinue were well armed. The better warriors wore brightly coloured and decorated clothing, horses, armour, helmets, shields and spears, axes and naturally swords and daggers. The warrior's status was often demonstrated by the quality of the equipment carried on his person, which may have been booty from a vanquished enemy or a gift from a leader.

The best Germanic warriors were professionals within these retinues (those in royal service being known as 'ring-givers'). They were long-haired swordsmen, well equipped by their wealthy masters; but in order to move quickly, they intentionally wore little armour. Their main weapons were, in addition to the long sword (*spatha*), axes, bows and arrows, spears and a short, single-edged dagger or a long dagger, the *scramasax*. The lance was the preferred weapon; while swords were probably less common, the *optimates* and the ring-givers certainly carried them.

Metal-forging technology and expert craftsmanship were much rarer among the Germanic tribes than in the Roman Empire, although there is evidence that the production and standardization of equipment had increased considerably in the first few centuries AD; the use of steel was known of, and *spathae* and javelin heads made of flexible steel were produced. In general, each man equipped himself as best he could. Of course, Alemannic production of sophisticated forged products, such as metal armour, helmets and swords, was certainly on a smaller scale than in Roman territory.

Bust of a young Germanic warrior, found at Welschbillig Castle, Germany. The castle was built on the site of a luxurious 4th-century AD Roman villa, which had 112 herms such as this one surrounding a decorated reflecting pool. This herm depicts a less Romanized young tribesman, who may have been captured from beyond the Rhine. The Welschbillig herms show distinctly different peoples, including Romans, Greeks, Celts, Germanics and deities too. It is believed that villa was imperial property, or housed the superintendent of the city walls. (Rheinisches Landesmuseum Trier; author's photo, courtesy of the museum)

In contrast to the Alemanni who formed the upper social classes, most Alemannic infantrymen had only a shield, with no armour or helmet, although after a victorious battle or raid they might be able to obtain these. Simple weapons like axes and knives were often made of non-forged iron. The less wealthy warriors might be armed with only a spear to accompany their shield. Basic clothing, made of wool, linen and wool-linen mix, comprised a tunic and trousers, over which a cloak was worn, sometimes made of fur. The long-sleeved, knee-length tunic found on Thorsberg moor in Germany, with openings at the wrists to allow the hands through, and tight hose with integrated socks were common to Romans and Germans alike, although Roman tunics were often embroidered. Sometimes, looser short-sleeved over-tunics were worn on top of the long-sleeved ones, and the lower legs were clad in wrap-around, puttee-like bindings. Waist belts, also used for holding weapons, were mainly Roman imports with decorative chip-carving (*Kerbschnitt*); they featured belt stiffeners, buckles and attachment rings for fastening a sword, purse and firesteel. These belts were very long. As among the Romans, the belts were universal items and indicated the wearer's status as a warrior.

During battle, Germanic princes fought mounted and commanded their single contingent, while nobles formed part of the cavalry contingent.

OPPOSING PLANS

GERMANIC

According to some modern authors, Chnodomar created his alliance as a defensive action to counter Julian's aggression, but this theory does not explain why he chose to engage the Roman army in pitched battle. This action finds little correspondence with the usual way that the Alemanni fought. As Elton points out, and noted previously, the Germans avoided pitched battles against the Romans whenever possible, commenting that '[t]heir almost inevitable defeat when engaged in open battles makes this understandable'. But the Alemannic victory over Barbatio, who possessed a larger force, the retreat of the Magister Peditum and the numerical superiority that the Germans possessed are more than convincing arguments to believe Ammianus, who stated that Chnodomar thought the moment had come to defeat the last Roman army defending Gaul. The idea that the Alemanni lacked a coherent plan and that Chnodomar exercised little effective leadership over the other Germanic rulers seems implausible.

The position maintained by Hough, who states that, given the lack of central authority throughout Alemannia, assembling raiding parties of more than 2,000 men would have involved some degree of leadership and planning, also lacks credibility. Chnodomar and the Alemanni tribes were already there and were already acting with some degree of coordination: all it required was for the promoter of the alliance (Chnodomar) to send messengers to the other Germanic leaders. Ammianus ascribes to Chnodomar a pre-existing king-like status over all the Alemanni, which is plausible, given he was the ruler who helped Constantius against Magnentius, and was certainly the most powerful Germanic ruler in the area. Moreover, it is possible that a coordinated effort had already been planned, if the Germans had received information regarding the intentions of Barbatio and his decision not to help the young *caesar* in any meaningful sense. For Constantius, the outcome of a direct clash between Julian and the Germanic tribes would be profitable whatever the result: if the Germanic tribes won, Julian's reputation (if he was able to even survive) would have been compromised forever. If Julian triumphed, his victory over the Alemanni would have been Constantius II's victory.

Nor did the Germans lack preparation. What their leaders were proposing was open battle, with their backs to the Rhine, and evidence of the unease this caused can be seen at the onset of the battle, when the infantry insisted that their leaders fight on foot, lest they should abandon them in the event

An advancing formation of Cornuti, Auxilia Palatina, as depicted on the Arch of Constantine in Rome, AD 313. This frieze, the best-preserved image of these elite troops, was sculpted some 45 years before the Battle of Argentoratum, in celebration of Constantine's campaign against Maxentius. Note the officer to the left wearing a muscled cuirass. (Manfred Beer)

that things did not go their way. This fear proved to be well founded, as events would prove that Chnodomar had in fact prepared an escape plan for just such an outcome.

The Germanic battle array

We know for sure that Chnodomar, determined to confront the Romans, deployed his army not far from the walls of Argentoratum (Strasbourg). The battlefield comprised a slightly sloping hill, several kilometres from the Rhine: it probably took place near the village of Oberhausbergen 5km north-west of the city. Near the village, the Romans had the first visual contact with the bulk of the enemy's army, which advanced in wedge formation, with the cavalry concentrated on the left wing, under the command of 'the wicked Chnodomar', a 2m-tall, obese giant, easily recognized by a flame-coloured tuft of hair (*flammeus torulus*) on his helmet and by the splendour of his weapons (Ammianus, XVI, 18.24).

The Alemannic infantry had positioned themselves on top of a rise. At the beginning, it seems they planned to be on the defensive. They had deployed most of their troops in their centre, divided into contingents (*pagi*) containing 800 men each. On the left flank – where the fighting would be the fiercest and where Chnodomar was positioned together with several *optimates* – the bulk of the Germanic cavalry were deployed, with light infantry dispersed throughout their formation in a supporting role – an old Germanic tactic, as used by Ariovistus against Caesar 400 years previously. The intention was for them to oppose the 600 Roman heavy cavalrymen (Catafractarii), which formed the weapon upon which Julian relied most. Serapio secured the right wing with a contingent of infantry lying in ambush in nearby woods. Here, anchored against a stream, the Alemanni set a trap for the Roman left wing by carefully constructing deep ditches hidden amongst reed beds, containing large numbers of warriors, who would be given the order to spring up suddenly during the clash. The ditches may have been little more than the bed of the Musau Stream, running alongside the Roman road. Libanius describes an aqueduct, a wood, a cane thicket and a piece of moorland, where the men were hiding for the ambush. The way in which Chnodomar had arrayed his forces may well provide evidence for the opinion that a traitor, sent by Barbatio, had informed the Alemannic king of Julian's battle plan.

ROMAN

Julian's decision to accept battle against an overwhelming force has been the subject of much debate by historians. Julian had many reasons to believe that he would defeat the Alemanni, whose morale was lower than that of the Romans. Given the differences in the two armies' training, arms and tactics, a pitched battle featuring comparable army sizes would almost certainly have played out in Rome's favour. According to Ammianus (XVIII, 2.14), 'The Romans, in this as in former campaigns, thought that the hardest part of their work was done once the enemy was located.' But the situation was not so simple, and Julian had several problems to overcome. In addition to the numerical superiority of the Germans, Chnodomar's army had already crossed the Rhine and was deployed on favourable terrain as Julian's army approached. Moreover, the Roman soldiers were tired: to reach the Alemannic horde and the battlefield, they had marched 34km. Chnodomar held the advantage in both numbers and terrain, and his warriors were brave

Detail of the helmet of a Cornuti infantryman from the Auxilia Palatina, Arch of Constantine in Rome. (Manfred Beer)

fighters. Notwithstanding this, two key factors pushed Julian into fighting a pitched battle. Firstly, there was the presence of an experienced commander in the form of the Magister Militum Severus, which countered the disadvantage that Julian himself was a relatively inexperienced general. Secondly, the ranks of Julian's army were filled with some of the Western Empire's most effective fighters. The experience and the solid battle organization of the Late Roman army would go a long way to countering any disadvantages.

The criticism by some historians that, if Ammianus' figures are accurate, the Alemanni could not have been halted after the flight of the Roman cavalry lacks credibility. Experienced and trained soldiers, even if fewer in number, can resist and hold off a less well trained yet larger enemy force. The warning by Vegetius (*De Re Militari*, III, 9.20) to avoid battle when one's numbers are inferior to those of the enemy is a simple, practical piece of military guidance, not a dictate to be applied by Roman commanders in all situations. At Faesulae (Fiesole) some 50 years later, the 20,000 troops of the Magister Militum Stilicho slaughtered the 400,000-strong army of the Germanic leader Radagaisus. The Roman army, even during the Late Empire period, was still superior in a pitched battle, and this factor was clearly understood by Julian.

According to Libanius, Julian could have prevented the Alemanni from crossing the Rhine. However, he preferred to fight, aware that a decisive victory on the battlefield would be seen as much more impressive by his soldiers and by the people of Gaul, who had been subject to years of civil war and devastation.

The Roman order of battle
Wucherpfennig has correctly identified the Roman battle array at Argentoratum (Strasbourg) as one of the seven standard Late-Roman battle formations, specifically the sixth model described by Vegetius, where the cavalry and the best troops were placed on one wing, and the other was protected by obstacles (Vegetius III, 20.4).

In Julian's army, the Auxilia Palatina spread out on the wings, while the legions were deployed in the centre. According to Ammianus, the greater part of the army was deployed opposite the front ranks of the barbarians (XVI,

A further detail of one of the heads of Cornuti infantryman from the Arch of Constantine. The Cornuti can be identified by two horns visible on the front of the helmet bowl, sometimes depicted as two metallic fittings, others times as bifurcated feather plumes. (Manfred Beer)

12.34). Julian deployed his infantry in two lines, spaced widely apart, each line several rows deep. In the centre of the first line were three of his five legions, including the army's standard (Libanius, *Oratio*, 139). In the centre, two lines were arrayed with a wide space between them, to extend across the full width of the deployment in order to avoid encirclement. The numerical superiority of the enemy led Julian to extend the depth of the first line, to absorb the greatest impact by the enemy. He therefore aimed to make it an impenetrable wall, and Ammianus uses a series of historical terms to describe its composition, speaking of *antepilani*, *hastati* and *primi ordines* (essentially, front-rank troops). Most probably, Ammianus intended to refer to a body of select warriors or officers, the *primi ordines* (a term once reserved for the centurions of greater experience and commanding the Cohortes I of Hastati, Principes and Triarii) placed in front of the other troops, in the first row, with other less experienced veterans behind them. The *hastati*, once one of the subdivisions of the army in the manipular cohorts, were now no longer a separate branch of service, but represented the homogeneously equipped and trained legionary, at the entry level of a career in a legion. Thus, the recruits were first Hastati and then, according to experience and passing through probation, transferred to the Principes and Triarii. The *antesignani* (literally, 'the men in front of the standards') were, according to Ammianus, arrayed several paces in front of the main formation in an effort to break up the enemy formations. The soldiers behind them (who were stationed behind the standards and in the extreme rear) in the Acies (i.e. in the formation, not in the whole army) were still called *postsignani* (Ammianus, XVI, 31).

A Cornuti infantryman throwing a lead-weighted dart (*plumbata*) from the Arch of Constantine. (Manfred Beer)

On the right of this main battle line were the elite Auxilia Palatina of Cornuti and Bracchiati.

Marching infantrymen of the Auxilium Palatinum of the Cornuti, Arch of Constantine, Rome. Note the plumes serving as a crest on the helmets, in contrast to the metal insignia visible on other Cornuti helmets on the same monument. (Manfred Beer)

They were arrayed in close combat order (*comminus*) as Ammianus makes clear (XVI, 12.42–43): 'Then the Alemanni, having beaten and scattered our cavalry, charged upon the front line of the infantry [*prima acies peditum*], supposing that their courage to resist was now lost and that they would therefore drive them back. But as soon as they came to close quarters … the Cornuti and the Bracchiati, toughened by long experience in fighting, at once intimidated them by their gestures, and raised their mighty battle-cry.'

The troops in the line furthest to the rear constituted the reserve, which would be engaged if the enemy broke through the front lines. Julian entrusted the reserve function to the second line, which was to engage only if the first line found itself in difficulty, but we do not know exactly which Auxilia units (repeatedly mentioned by Ammianus during the battle) manned the first and second lines. We do know that in the centre of the second line Julian placed his elite units, such as the legion of the Primani, but considering that the *caesar* had spent the previous winter recruiting soldiers, it is possible that many had only just completed training and therefore lacked any form of military experience.

On the right wing, where the ground was flatter, Julian's entire cavalry force was deployed, with light skirmishers in front of them, to disrupt the enemy before the heavy cavalry, consisting of the Catafractarii (possibly the Equites Catafractarii Ambianenses), launched their shock charge. On the left side, slightly to the rear of the front line, was Severus, accompanied by other infantry units. The left wing was protected by marshy ground around an aqueduct over the Musau Stream.

Julian, with his *comitatus* of 200 guards (the other 160 bodyguards were probably dispatched to support the cavalry), positioned himself between the Roman lines, on the side of the cavalry, positioned more probably towards the right than the centre. For a considerable period of time, Julian encouraged his troops, reminding them not to get carried away if the enemy's ranks were broken, and to avoid pursuing the enemy too quickly.

THE BATTLE OF ARGENTORATUM

Just before the two armies clashed, cries rose up along the length of the Alemannic battle line. These shouts, however, were not the *barritus* war cry, but cries of indignation towards the Germanic commanders, who were obliged by the foot soldiers to dismount from their horses to prevent them, in case of difficulty or rout, from abandoning the common warriors to their fate. Chnodomar himself led by example, dismounting from his horse, followed by the rulers and commanders.

The sound of blaring trumpets heralded the advance of the two sides and the beginning of the battle, the first act in which was the launching of javelins on both sides. Julian pushed forward both his infantry and cavalry, unaware of the danger that lay in store for Severus on the Roman left. The Germans advanced more quickly, paying little attention to maintaining a tight formation, and rushed to attack the Romans using their javelins, lunging at their bodies; according to Ammianus, 'they gnashed their teeth hideously and raged beyond their usual manner, their flowing hair made a terrible sight, and a kind of madness shone from their eyes.'

In earlier times, such as those during the invasions of the Cimbri and Teutones (113–101 BC), such a spectacle would have terrified the Roman legions, causing them to rout as happened at Arausio (Orange) and Noreia (location unknown). But now, in the middle of the 4th century AD, the multi-ethnic composition of Roman armies and their familiarity with confronting frenzied barbarian warriors allowed the imperial troops to support each other with cold-blooded nerves. The legionaries fought protecting their heads

A map of the area in which the Battle of Argentoratum took place, showing the topography of the terrain. (Public domain)

with their shields held high and keeping their opponents at bay with their swords or by thrusting javelins back in turn.

On the Roman left, the barbarian enemy began to spring their ambush, and Severus had to deal with swarms of adversaries who suddenly emerged from the ground. But the premature fury of some of the barbarians betrayed them, with some emerging from their hiding places too soon, which gave warning to the Roman commander of a trap. Severus managed to stop his men before they had advanced too far, and found themselves under attack from two directions – from the front by the bulk of the Alemannic army, and on the left flank by the ambushing force. Nevertheless, the Roman left wing had to resist the impetus of a disproportionate number of enemy warriors. The mêlée that arose following the meeting of the two sides involved infantry and cavalry troops in equal measure, and provoked a long series of back and forth movements, during which both sides advanced then retreated in turn.

During the first phase of the clash, Severus' wing found itself in difficulty and it was on this side that Julian concentrated his attention. Whilst riding to his subordinate along with 200 bodyguards, the *caesar* encouraged his soldiers with stirring words along the Roman line, and ordered them to fight in a less rigid order to avoid being surrounded by the barbarians, oblivious to the projectiles falling all around him. At the same time, when he saw a unit advancing into the enemy line and risking isolation, he called it back, urging the troops to keep their line and not to be carried away in the heat of battle. He may have fought only with his words, but he knew they were more effective than wielding his sword and entering the fray.

Julian's incitements had some effect, and the Romans succeeded in pushing forward deeply with their left wing. They managed to break the

The site of the Roman camp prior to the Battle of Argentoratum, showing the route of the ancient road going to Tres Tabernae (Saverne). (Jasper Oorthuys © Karwansaray Publishers)

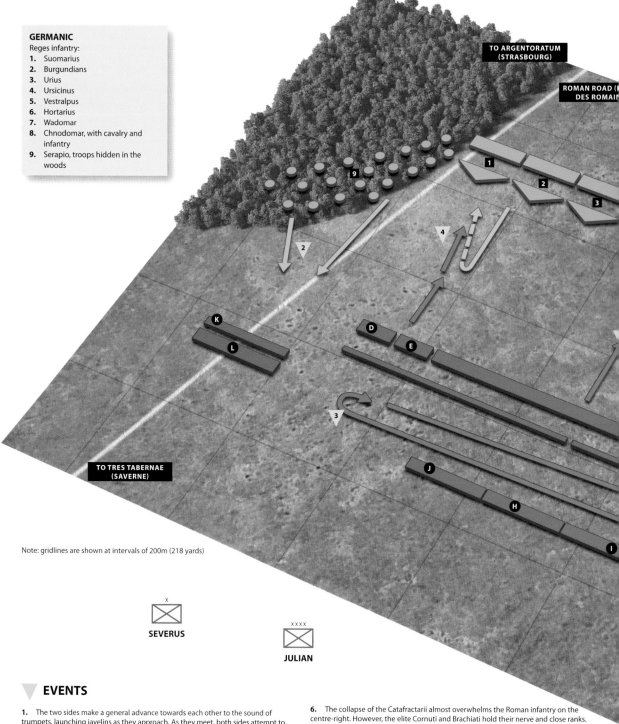

GERMANIC

Reges infantry:
1. Suomarius
2. Burgundians
3. Urius
4. Ursicinus
5. Vestralpus
6. Hortarius
7. Wadomar
8. Chnodomar, with cavalry and infantry
9. Serapio, troops hidden in the woods

TO ARGENTORATUM (STRASBOURG)

ROMAN ROAD (
DES ROMAIN

TO TRES TABERNAE
(SAVERNE)

Note: gridlines are shown at intervals of 200m (218 yards)

SEVERUS

JULIAN

⚊ EVENTS

1. The two sides make a general advance towards each other to the sound of trumpets, launching javelins as they approach. As they meet, both sides attempt to gain the upper hand on the field, advancing and retreating in turn.

2. Some of Serapio's troops hidden in the forest move forward and engage Severus' troops on the Roman left flank, losing the element of surprise for any future ambush. Many of Serapio's troops remain hidden in the woods.

3. Julian and his bodyguards ride to the Roman left to support Severus, encouraging the Roman main line as he moves across the battlefield.

4. The left wing of the Roman line manages to advance forward, breaking the line of the Alemanni and gradually forcing them back to the raised ground behind.

5. On the Roman right, the heavy cavalry of the Catafractarii charges the cavalry and infantry on Chnodomar's left wing. Chnodomar's light infantry cause havoc, inserting themselves between the Catafractarii and slaughtering horses and riders. The Roman cavalry begins to panic and retreats in disorder, crashing into the Roman infantry in the centre-right.

6. The collapse of the Catafractarii almost overwhelms the Roman infantry on the centre-right. However, the elite Cornuti and Brachiati hold their nerve and close ranks.

7. Julian returns to the right wing, and attempts to prevent his cavalry from being routed. Zosimus' account of the battle indicates that he was not successful in this, and that the Catafractarii played no further role of significance in the battle. Others indicate that Julian did manage to rally some of his cavalry, and some form of order was restored to the rear of the Roman lines. The Germanic cavalry may then have moved to attack Severus on the Roman left flank.

8. With the Roman cavalry overwhelmed, the Germanic infantry push forward their attack on the Roman right, certain that their numerical superiority will sooner or later break the line.

9. The Roman right wing is defended by the Gallic auxiliary regiments of Cornuti and Brachiati, and the experienced units of the Auxilia Palatina. After repeated attacks by the Alemanni, the Roman line here is eventually broken. The Romans are pushed back here almost to their rear camp, until the Batavi and those guarding the camp manage to hold and then push back the Alemanni.

THE OPENING MOVES

The battle began with both sides advancing and launching javelins against each other. Although the Romans on their left wing managed to push the Alemanni back onto the higher ground, the Germanic infantry and cavalry on the opposite wing overcame the Roman heavy cavalry, causing it to flee in disorder. The personal intervention of Julian on the Roman right managed to stop the rout.

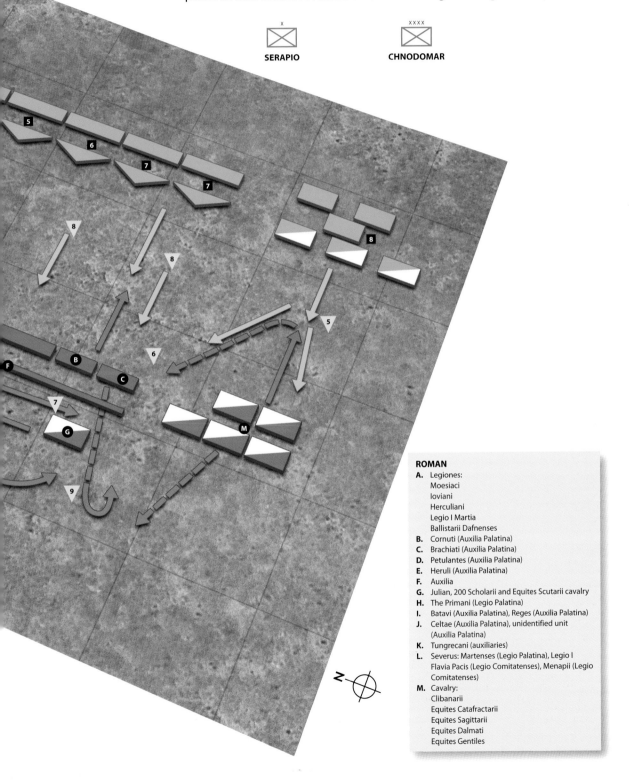

SERAPIO

CHNODOMAR

ROMAN
A. Legiones:
Moesiaci
Ioviani
Herculiani
Legio I Martia
Ballistarii Dafnenses
B. Cornuti (Auxilia Palatina)
C. Brachiati (Auxilia Palatina)
D. Petulantes (Auxilia Palatina)
E. Heruli (Auxilia Palatina)
F. Auxilia
G. Julian, 200 Scholarii and Equites Scutarii cavalry
H. The Primani (Legio Palatina)
I. Batavi (Auxilia Palatina), Reges (Auxilia Palatina)
J. Celtae (Auxilia Palatina), unidentified unit (Auxilia Palatina)
K. Tungrecani (auxiliaries)
L. Severus: Martenses (Legio Palatina), Legio I Flavia Pacis (Legio Comitatenses), Menapii (Legio Comitatenses)
M. Cavalry:
Clibanarii
Equites Catafractarii
Equites Sagittarii
Equites Dalmati
Equites Gentiles

Another view of the area of the Roman camp at Argentoratum, and the ancient road to Tres Tabernae (Saverne). (Jasper Oorthuys © Karwansaray Publishers)

Alemanni lines, gradually gain ground and begin to pursue them along the slope of the hill.

Things did not go so well on the opposite Roman wing, however. An unforeseen collapse of the Roman right by the heavy cavalry of the Catafractarii – the very asset on which Julian was counting – took place. The heavy Roman cavalry had charged against the Germanic left, where the barbarians, as noted earlier, had placed their light infantry mixed in with their cavalry. These Alemannic infantry infiltrated themselves among the Catafractarii, picked off the Roman horses from below and then dispatched their unseated riders.

But the efforts of the Alemanni were not the only factors involved in the collapse. The Clibanarii, already unnerved by these tactics, witnessed the wounding of their leader (*rector*), and then one of their fellow riders at the front of the fray was thrown forward over the neck of his horse, and subsequently crushed by the weight of its armoured body: this was enough to send them into a panic, and they turned their backs on the enemy and fled in disorder.

As they fell back, the lead elements of the Clibanarii ran into the advance of those behind them, arresting their impetus and nullifying the kinetic energy of the entire contingent. In their haste to escape, the fleeing cavalrymen crashed into the Roman infantry on the right. The Roman infantry on this flank even risked being overwhelmed by their rout. The infantry, however, maintained its rank formation. Thanks to the steely resolve of the Roman infantry officers and the cast-iron determination and training of the elite Cornuti and Bracchiati units, the infantry here were able to close ranks and

establish a barrier against their own retreating cavalry, before even the enemy had reached them, and diverted the passage of their flight.

According to Ammianus, the personal intervention of the *caesar* halted the Roman cavalry's retreat and returned them to the fray. Julian spurred his horse on and, crossing the entire battlefield, placed himself before the cavalry 'like a kind of barrier,' even risking being overwhelmed. He would indeed have been overwhelmed, had not one of the tribunes of the Clibanarii noticed his standard, a purple dragon (*purpureum signum draconis*), atop a long pole carried by one of the members of his escort. The presence of the supreme commander shamed the officer into action, and, pale in face, he turned his horse around and returned to the fight, an example immediately imitated by those under his command.

One of the criticisms that Julian's detractors level against him is his wordiness, and the young *caesar* was at least consistent in this regard on the field of battle, according to the available sources, addressing his fleeing troops thus: 'Whither are we fleeing, my most valiant men? Do you know not that flight never leads to safety, but shows the folly of a useless effort? Let us return to our companions, to be at least sharers in their coming glory, if it is without consideration that we are abandoning them as they fight for their country.'

The truth of the matter is that it would be almost impossible for any commander to halt the flight of a heavy cavalry unit, which would not stop until it found a major obstacle in its path and which would have been able to hear next to nothing of such words due to the thundering of hooves on the ground and the clanging of metal parts made by both horse and

The battlefield today, at Oberhausbergen, looking north from the Roman road to Strasbourg (Argentoratum). This was behind the Roman lines during the battle. (Jasper Oorthuys © Karwansaray Publishers)

rider. As a result, the present authors believe that, from that moment, the Catafractarii no longer played any significant role in the battle. The later source of Zosimus supports this, stating that there was no way of bringing them back into the fight (III, 68):

> [Julian] possessed a regiment of six hundred horse, which were well disciplined, and in whose valour and experience he so confided, that he ventured great part of his hopes upon their performances. Indeed when the battle commenced, the whole army attacked the enemy with all the resolution they could show; but some time afterwards, though the Roman army had considerably the advantage, these were the only troops that fled, and left their station so dishonourably, that when Caesar rode up to them with a small party, and called them back to a share of the victory, he could not by any means prevail on them to turn.

Sometimes, strange as it may seem, we are led to give more credit to later sources, untouched by the influence of propaganda, than to contemporary ones.

Delbrück also concurs with this viewpoint, and suggest that stories of a commander miraculously rallying a unit only really occur when fresh units come into play. He also highlights the fact that Ammianus states that Roman infantry reserves entered the fray to engage the Alemannic cavalry. Delbrück's view is that only a part of the Roman cavalry remained near the battlefield and re-engaged at a point in which it was clear that the battle had been won; this is consistent with Ammianus' vague description of the Roman cavalry's return.

In one or another way, however, according to our sources, the *caesar* managed to bring them once again into contact with the enemy, whose cavalry, meanwhile, had ridden out of sight, probably passing to the opposite side of the battlefield to attack the rear of the advancing Severus. Ammianus tells us nothing more about the Alemannic cavalry from this moment onwards.

The Catafractarii took up position behind the lines of their infantry, from where they returned to the fight. For his part, Julian would not easily forgive his favourite arm, if what Zosimus tells us is true: according to the latter, on the evening that followed the battle, the *caesar* obliged the Clibanarii to walk around the Roman camp dressed as women.

Even if the young *caesar* had managed to reform the heavy cavalry line, the damage was now done: the right flank of the Roman infantry had been left without cover for enough time to allow the Alemannic infantry to attack the first Roman line on its flank. Encouraged by the success of their

The *stela* (monument stone) of Klaudianus Ingenuus of the Numerus Equitum Catafractorum Seniorum, from Lugdunum (Lyon), second quarter of the 4th century AD. Klaudianus Ingenuus is represented on his *stela* armed with a *contus* (wooden cavalry lance) and a long coat of scale armour, a plumed helmet and boots, riding a horse without protective armour. The Catafractarii listed in the *Notitia Dignitatum* and that fought with Julian at Argentoratum may have been different to the Clibanarii units and lacked horse protection, but this constituted an exception. (Andrea Salimbeti, after Esperandieu)

Another view of the Argentoratum battlefield. (Jasper Oorthuys © Karwansaray Publishers)

cavalry, the barbarians launched themselves with growing confidence against their adversaries, in the certainty that their numerical superiority would sooner or later break the Roman resistance.

The Alemannic infantry let out a huge roar and advanced towards the Roman line. But the line in this sector was manned by the Gallic auxiliary regiments of the Cornuti and Bracchiati, experienced units of the Auxilia Palatina, which were not about to be intimidated by anyone. On the contrary, they also had a few tricks up their sleeves for creating turmoil among the enemy. In the middle of the battle, they emitted their famous *barritus* war cry, a sound that rose from a low murmur, gradually grew louder, and then turned into a roar, growing progressively louder 'like waves dashing against the cliffs'.

It is also possible, however, that the aforementioned Auxilia were part of the second line and that they intervened to provide the former with strength in numbers to reinforce its flank. With the passing of time, the combatants involved in the mêlée became caught up in the blind rage of battle and, in the dusty murk that had risen around them, they milled their weapons and hurled javelins without aiming at any specific target. The space between fighters was shrinking minute by minute and for each soldier, jostled by his fellow soldiers and his enemies, it became increasingly difficult to maintain balance. Gradually the imperial troops made good use of this lack of space, closing up their ranks further and creating impenetrable tortoise formations with their shields.

The Germanic warriors attacked the closed ranks of the Romans several times over. The Alemanni tried everything to break up the enemy formations, storming them with their swords and raining all sorts of missiles down on

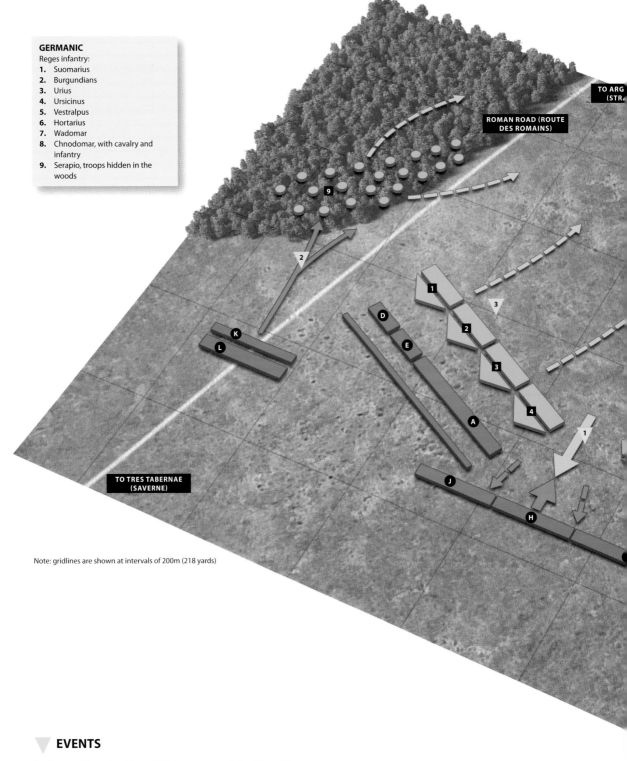

GERMANIC

Reges infantry:

1. Suomarius
2. Burgundians
3. Urius
4. Ursicinus
5. Vestralpus
6. Hortarius
7. Wadomar
8. Chnodomar, with cavalry and infantry
9. Serapio, troops hidden in the woods

TO ARG
(STR.

ROMAN ROAD (ROUTE DES ROMAINS)

TO TRES TABERNAE
(SAVERNE)

Note: gridlines are shown at intervals of 200m (218 yards)

EVENTS

1. A group of Germanic nobles and their clansmen manage to break through the centre of the Roman first line and reach the second Roman battle line, clashing with the Legio Palatina of the Primani, which manages to halt their advance.

2. On the Roman left wing, Severus moves forward and routs the Germanic troops in the woods, preventing any attempt at an ambush, and attacking the Germanic line from the flank.

3. The bulk of the Germanic force is gradually being enveloped by the Romans, compressing the centre. The Germanic line begins to collapse, and Chnodomar's warriors begin to flee for their lives.

4. Julian continues to exert pressure from the flanks, and a general pursuit begins as the Alemanni attempt to reach the safety of the Rhine River.

x

SEVERUS

xxxx

JULIA

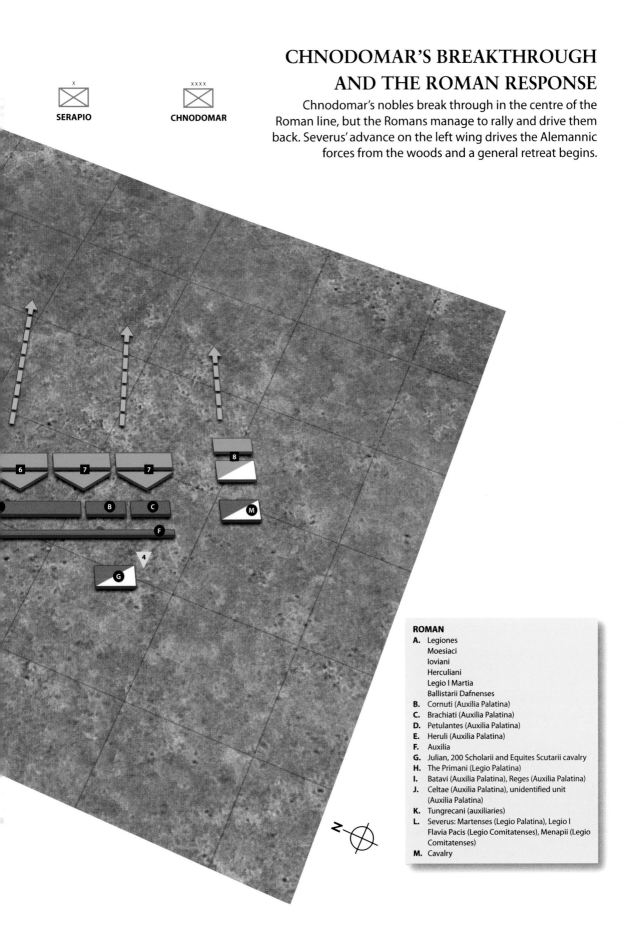

CHNODOMAR'S BREAKTHROUGH AND THE ROMAN RESPONSE

Chnodomar's nobles break through in the centre of the Roman line, but the Romans manage to rally and drive them back. Severus' advance on the left wing drives the Alemannic forces from the woods and a general retreat begins.

ROMAN
A. Legiones
  Moesiaci
  Ioviani
  Herculiani
  Legio I Martia
  Ballistarii Dafnenses
B. Cornuti (Auxilia Palatina)
C. Brachiati (Auxilia Palatina)
D. Petulantes (Auxilia Palatina)
E. Heruli (Auxilia Palatina)
F. Auxilia
G. Julian, 200 Scholarii and Equites Scutarii cavalry
H. The Primani (Legio Palatina)
I. Batavi (Auxilia Palatina), Reges (Auxilia Palatina)
J. Celtae (Auxilia Palatina), unidentified unit (Auxilia Palatina)
K. Tungrecani (auxiliaries)
L. Severus: Martenses (Legio Palatina), Legio I Flavia Pacis (Legio Comitatenses), Menapii (Legio Comitatenses)
M. Cavalry

The possible location where Chnodomar and his mixed cavalry and infantry were positioned at the outset of the Battle of Argentoratum, viewed from the Roman perspective. (Jasper Oorthuys © Karwansaray Publishers)

them, from simple light javelins to heavier and longer lances, both shaped-head and simpler iron-tipped versions. When they were able to open up a gap in the lines, they used their greater physical strength to push their way through the enemy ranks, sometimes even clambering over the top of the shields of the Romans.

But the Roman front line held, inflicting heavy losses on the Germans, who threw their bodies against the massed Roman spears. The Bracchiati and Cornuti held fast. Those who had been wounded found the strength to get back on their feet and resume their clash with the enemy, while the officers did their best to maintain the cohesion of their units in the face of the barbarian onslaught. Despite the appearance of some gaps in the line, into which some groups of Germanic warriors penetrated, the Auxilia units used their experience to steady the separate wings in the battle array.

Nonetheless, the Alemannic pressure was too strong for them to resist indefinitely, and the Batavi and the Regi, two further units of the Auxilia Palatina, came to their aid from the left wing, reinforcing the line and allowing the Roman battle line to push forward once again. However, the barbarians also knew how to defend successfully, and when each was exhausted, he gave way to a fresher companion, and rested his left knee on the ground, while continuing to ward off any enemy soldier who approached using his spear.

The Batavi sustained the assault of the superior Germanic infantry, which had broken through the Roman first line. Pushed back to the hill where the Roman camp had been set up, the Batavi were reinforced there by the camp guards and repulsed and broke the enemy.

By now, it had become a challenge between discipline and impetus, between order and brute force. But no fighter was willing to yield any ground,

each motivated by the valiant behaviour of his fellow fighters alongside him. The balance, however, shifted again in favour of the Alemanni when a group of nobles, followed by their respective retinues, managed to break through the centre of the Roman line and reach the second Roman line. There they ran into the Legio Palatina of the Primani, which was able to halt them.

The hill behind which Serapio's Germanic troops assembled to ambush Severus' soldiers on the Roman left flank. (Jasper Oorthuys © Karwansaray Publishers)

Meanwhile, on the Roman left wing, Severus had managed to force out and disperse the Alemannic troops hidden in the woods, dissipating the threat of an ambush, and moved on to attack the barbarians from the rear. A large number of Germanic warriors found themselves bottled in, slowly being surrounded and pressed on every side, while the Romans reconstituted their lines. The front line, now extended on the left side with the return of Severus' victorious troops, began to push back the Germans, while those who were bottled in were gradually decimated. The bulk of the barbarians were now trapped in an increasingly narrow and compact Roman pincer, with the troops on the wings methodically being cut to pieces and those in the middle so tightly packed in that they could not move. As often happened to barbarian armies in the field, who were as quick to anger as they were to lose heart, within the space of a few minutes their mood changed and warriors who had fought with joyful expressions now thought of nothing else but flight, each saving himself, without heeding the orders of the barbarian commanders. Their flight unnerved the companions to their rear, who themselves turned away from the enemy, provoking a general rout of the barbarian army. At this moment, the Germanic line underwent a general collapse: panic took hold, and warriors broke ranks and fled for their lives.

The Romans found they now had easy targets on which to vent their full fury. They chased the backs of the fleeing barbarians, who had given up the

THE GERMANIC CHARGE AGAINST THE ROMAN PRIMANI SHIELD WALL (PP. 68–69)

A decisive moment in the Battle of Argentoratum came when a group of Germanic nobles and their respective clansmen managed to break through the centre of the Roman lines and reach the Roman second line, where it came up against the Legio Palatina of Primani. The members of this legion knew how to fight in close formation better than any other: holding their ground, standing tall and protecting each other with their shields like a Greek phalanx. The Romans held their position, and managed to lunge at the barbarians with their javelins and slash at them with their swords, inflicting injury and death. The Germans, for their part, continued to attack the 'human fortress' in an uncoordinated manner, spurring each other one and without taking care to protect each other or protect their battle line. The Alemanni obstinately continued the assault on the legionaries even clambering over the corpses of their fellow barbarians to get

at the Romans, the moans of the wounded men and the futility of their efforts failing to demoralize them, but still they were unable to break the Primani line.

Here we see the barbarians (**1**) attempting to crack the closed Roman tortoise formation (**2**), but in vain. Ammianus suggests that many Alemannic infantrymen were armed with swords (*gladii*, **3**), while others wielded daggers and axes (**4**): 'but the savages … hacked with repeated strokes of their swords at the close-jointed array of shields, which protected our men like a tortoise-formation … Yet darts [*spicula*] and javelins [*missilia*] did not cease to fly, with showers of iron-tipped arrows [*arundines ferratae*], although at close quarters also blade [*mucro*] clashed on blade and breastplates [*loricae*]) were cleft with the sword' (XVI, 12.44–46). Among the Alemanni, poor men often served as archers.

fight, and many even managed to snatch the javelins from their enemies and plunge them into their owners, and severing heads that, Ammianus states, dangled inert from their torsos. In short, the ground was covered with the dead, but also with the wounded, who begged companions and enemies to finish them; the soil was filled with blood throughout the battlefield, making the ground slippery under the feet of pursuers and fugitives. Many died trampled by their own companions, in an expanse of abandoned helmets and shields. It was said that the swords of the Romans were blunted by large amounts of helmets and *loricae* they struck, creating piles of corpses that eventually even obstructed the barbarian escape routes. But the victors did not give up and carried on slaughtering the defeated with their daggers.

The fleeing Alemanni converged on the Rhine, hoping to find refuge in the river. Many were not quick enough to do so: chased to the Rhine by the Roman cavalry and infantry, they were struck down as they ran. A large number attempted to swim across the river, but many drowned, hit by darts or weighed down by their armour; even those that could swim perished in the swirling waters. Julian had to instruct the tribunes to halt the pursuit on the banks of the river, to avoid the dangers of its waters for his men. From that point onwards, the Romans stood on its banks and targeted the escaping Germans, throwing javelins at those reeling in its waters trying to reach the eastern shore. Many who did not know how to swim clung to those who did, facilitating the work of the Roman javelin throwers, while others tried to float on the shields, avoiding the currents; 'And if any of them by his speed escaped this death, he would sink to the bottom of the river through the weight of his struggling body.' Soon the Rhine became a red-tinged flow in which hundreds of bodies were dragged away by the current, while those

The location of Julian's army at Argentoratum, seen from the Germanic right flank, where Serapio's Germanic infantry prepared an ambush for Severus' forces. (Jasper Oorthuys © Karwansaray Publishers)

THE SURRENDER OF CHNODOMAR (PP. 72–73)

Each of the Germanic kings, princes and warlords at Argentoratum had around him his own *comitatus* or retinue, bound to their sovereign or ruler by a code of loyalty. An example of this code is provided by the episode described by Ammianus relating to the capture of Chnodomar (1), the Alemannic king, at the end of the battle. The defeated king, accompanied by 200 of his men, had attempted to escape but was cut off and surrounded by the Romans. Chnodomar 'was driven to the utmost fear and surrendered of his own accord, coming out alone; and his attendants, two hundred in number, with three of his closest friends (2), thinking it a disgrace to survive their king, or not to die for their king if an emergency required it, gave themselves up to be made prisoners'.

Did the Alemannic princes and rulers wear elaborate helmets of the Baldenheim type, as is so often shown in reconstructions? We cannot exclude that some highly precious examples of decorated spangenhelm were already being produced in the second half of the 4th century AD. However, recent archaeological work has shown that this type of spangenhelm was widespread only in the 5th century AD and in all probability was first produced in Roman workshops and then adopted by the Germanic princes. Chnodomar's magnificent helmet, sporting a red crest, was therefore in all probability of the Late Roman heavy cavalry type, as we have chosen to show here in this reconstruction of his surrender.

of the Germanic leaders, weighed down by their more elaborate armour, rested on its bed.

But Chnodomar was not among the leaders who had escaped across the river. The supreme commander of the Alemanni, the man who more than any other had wanted war, had concealed himself among the corpses on the battlefield and then, when the Romans had moved to the banks of the Rhine, had covered his face with mud so as not to be recognized. Accompanied by several bodyguards, he had returned towards his camp on horseback, seeking to reach one of several boats he had hidden further downriver in preparation for every eventuality. With these boats he intended to return to his territories. But Chnodomar struggled to find the place where they had been moored and ended up heading along the riverbank, on marshy ground, where his horse stopped suddenly, causing his saddle to slip. It was then that

A panoramic montage of the Argentoratum battlefield, viewed from the Germanic right. (Jasper Oorthuys © Karwansaray Publishers)

a tribune from a Roman patrol dispatched to search for Chnodomar spotted him. The Alemannic king was able to retire to a wooded hill (near modern Hohenheim) with around 200 men, where he was able to hold out against the Roman attacks, aided by the forest cover.

However, Chnodomar realized that time was running out and he decided to exit the forest alone, surrendering himself to an imperial officer without saying a word. Three companions immediately followed him out of the woods, 'thinking it a disgrace to survive their king, or not to die for their king if an emergency required it', according to Ammianus.

Meanwhile, the massacre on the banks of the river continued. Julian put an end to it by ordering the trumpets to be blown once again, and his troops reluctantly complied, returning to their new encampment, which the *caesar*

A Late Roman military horse, Villa Romana del Tellaro, Sicily. The traditional Roman four-cornered saddle was abandoned from the start of the 4th century AD in favour of the raised arch saddle, influenced by the Steppe horsemen such as the Alans, Sarmatians and Huns. (Dipartimento dei beni culturali e dell'identità siciliana; authors' photo)

had ordered established on the banks of the Rhine. There was no time to fortify it with wall or ditch, and for those resting there after the turmoil of battle, the only protection provided was by a cordon of standing soldiers with their shields before them.

The victors counted their own dead and, surprisingly, discovered they had lost only 243 soldiers and four tribunes, for whom Ammianus (XVI, 12.63) is even able to give names for three of them: Bainobaudes, *tribunus* of the Cornuti; and Laipso and Innocentius, commanders of the Clibanarii. The fourth was a supernumerary tribune whose name remained unknown.

Julian wished to immediately grasp the scale of his victory and sent men out to count the fallen enemy, too, but given the great number of corpses dispersed in the current of the river, they found it almost impossible to provide an accurate number. On the battlefield alone, however, 6,000 bodies were identified (about one-third of Chnodomar's army) according to Ammianus, although Libanius gives a figure of 8,000. The figure of 60,000 provided by Zosimus is an obvious error on the part of a later copyist. The *caesar* finally called for Chnodomar, who was brought before him at the end of the day. The Alemannic king, so proud and provocative at the head of his army, was now downcast and humbled. He threw himself on his knees and begged Julian for forgiveness in his own tongue. The *caesar* assured him of his safety and ordered him to be sent back to Rome in chains for the emperor to decide his fate.

The great Roman victory, perhaps one of the last clear triumphs that the empire achieved on the battlefield against an external enemy, exalted the soldiers to such an extent that they acclaimed their commander as an *augustus*. Aware of the extent of their gesture, which constituted a possible challenge to the power of Constantius II, Julian hurried to quell their enthusiasm and shied away by saying it was a 'charge he did not hope for nor wanted to achieve'. Only three years later, however, annoyed by the denigration to which he was subjected at the imperial court, he would indulge the whims of the army and accept the investiture.

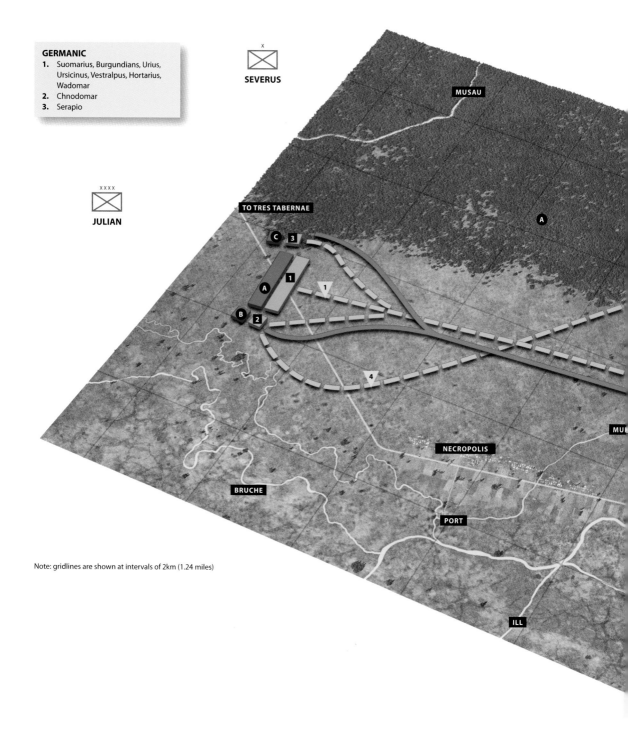

GERMANIC
1. Suomarius, Burgundians, Urius, Ursicinus, Vestralpus, Hortarius, Wadomar
2. Chnodomar
3. Serapio

x
SEVERUS

MUSAU

xxxx
JULIAN

TO TRES TABERNAE

C 3
A 1
B
2

A

1

4

NECROPOLIS

MU

BRUCHE

PORT

ILL

Note: gridlines are shown at intervals of 2km (1.24 miles)

 EVENTS

1. The Germanic forces begin their retreat from the battlefield, pursued by the Roman infantry and cavalry.

2. Germanic warriors reach the marshy ground bordering the Rhine, hoping to escape by swimming across the river to its eastern bank.

3. Julian instructs the tribunes to stop the pursuit on the banks of the Rhine River, to avoid risking Roman lives in its fast-flowing waters. Instead, the Romans rain missiles down on the fleeing Germanic troops trying to reach the eastern shore. Many of Chnodomar's men drown, weighed down by their clothing and armour, or are killed by Roman missiles or darts.

4. Chnodomar, his face besmirched with mud to avoid being recognized, has retreated on horseback with several bodyguards to the Germanic camp. He plans to return by water to home territory, but is unable to locate the boats that had previously been hidden. While passing along the bank of the river, he is thrown from the saddle and is spotted by Roman soldiers.

5. Chnodomar flees to a wooded hill (near modern Hohenheim) with 200 of his men, where he is able to hold off the attacks by his Roman pursuers using the cover of the trees. Realizing defeat is inevitable, he surrenders himself without resistance to an imperial officer.

6. Meanwhile, the massacre on the banks of the river continues. Julian puts an end to it with a trumpet signal, and his soldiers return to their newly established camp, on the banks of the Rhine.

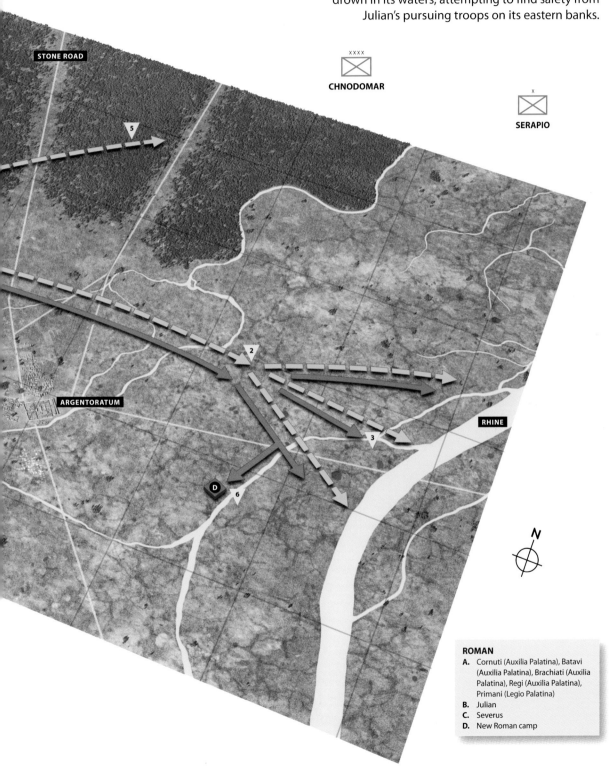

THE RETREAT TO THE RHINE

Once Chnodomar's Germanic forces began to collapse, his warriors lost their nerve, and a headlong retreat to the Rhine began. Many would drown in its waters, attempting to find safety from Julian's pursuing troops on its eastern banks.

STONE ROAD

CHNODOMAR

SERAPIO

ARGENTORATUM

RHINE

N

ROMAN
A. Cornuti (Auxilia Palatina), Batavi (Auxilia Palatina), Brachiati (Auxilia Palatina), Regi (Auxilia Palatina), Primani (Legio Palatina)
B. Julian
C. Severus
D. New Roman camp

AFTERMATH

JULIAN'S FOLLOW-ON OPERATIONS

Julian claimed to have liberated slaves and spoil from the Alemanni, not those taken by the Germans while serving the Roman emperor, but those taken at the time of the sack of Colonia Agrippinensis (Cologne). In the edicts issued by Constantius, it is recorded that Chnodomar was presented to the emperor, and that Constantius himself planned the Roman battle dispositions and put the barbarians to flight, despite (writes Ammianus) the fact that he was 40 days' travel from the site of the battle. Julian's name is not mentioned at all, notwithstanding the extreme deference that the *caesar* had shown towards his imperial cousin. Chnodomar's contrition and repentance saw him imprisoned in Rome in the Castra Peregrina on the Caelius Mountain, where he died not long afterwards. His disappearance from the chessboard, at least, deprived the Alemanni of the only ruler who had sufficient authority to gather all the others under a single authority. Confusion and disorientation reigned among the barbarians now, and Julian was aware that he should take advantage of it to give more substance to his victory. If in southern Gaul he could rely on the alliance with Vadomarus, a king who had respected his pact with Constantius, in the north there was still much to do to settle the situation along the border: although many local kings had not participated in the battle, they had still sent warrior contingents to support Chnodomar.

Now that the risk of fighting a coalition was no longer present, the *caesar* could face down the independent *reguli* one by one, bringing the war directly to their territories, beyond the Rhine. Indeed, the Battle of Argentoratum would be the only one Julian fought in his five-year stay in Gaul. Both the barbarians and also the Roman commanders preferred surprise attacks and ambushes to pitched battles, minimizing the risk of losing soldiers, who were always difficult to replace.

The Roman leader ordered all the fallen of the battle to be buried in mass graves, without distinction as to their origin, sent prisoners and loot to Divodurum (Metz) and then hurried to Mogontiacum (Mainz). Then, just north of the mouth of the Main River, he built a bridge of boats as rapidly as Julius Caesar had built his for his first raid east of the river, and penetrated the insidious territory. But not everything went smoothly: it was by now the end of September, and it had been a long campaigning season. The soldiers had had enough of marching and fighting, and were longing to return to winter quarters, believing that they deserved their rest. Even the failure to

Bust of the Emperor Julian, in chalcedony, 4th century AD. Julian is wearing a cloak (*chlamys*) fastened with a *fibula* on his left shoulder, and has a richly decorated bracelet (*armilla*) round his right wrist. His cloak's hem is lined with gems. His pupils were probably inlaid. The groove around his head is for attaching a metal diadem. (State Hermitage Museum, St Petersburg; authors' photo, courtesy of the museum)

share the campaign's spoils aroused discontent. Julian had to muster all his dialectical ability to persuade them to follow him, and was even threatened with a possible military mutiny.

His arrival caused real surprise among the Alemanni who had settled on the Main, and at first they could do little other than sue for peace. But then their leaders regained their courage and challenged the *caesar*, telling him to retire to imperial territory or prepare for conflict. However, Julian had gained great confidence from his victory at Argentoratum and did not allow himself to be intimidated. One night, he ordered 800 of his men to cross the river in small boats and to land behind the enemy warriors threatening his left flank. The Alemanni thus found themselves at risk of being caught in a pincer movement and had to withdraw into the hills beyond the Main, abandoning their territory to Roman devastation. The imperial army was able to put the region to the flame unmolested, travelling for almost 5km to the edges of the Hercynia Silva (Hercynian Forest), in the hilly area today known as Spessart, between north-western Bavaria and the southern part of Hesse. Julian's men encountered no resistance but had to halt when they found their path obstructed by felled trunks of oak, ash and fir. The snow now began to whiten the tops of the mountains, but it was not this that made Julian decide to bring the campaign to an end. He withdrew, but only across the Main to rebuild an old fort that had been constructed two and a half centuries earlier by the emperor Trajan. Its location is still the subject of debate, but its presence was enough to induce the three rulers who controlled the region to swear an act of obedience, even undertaking to supply the

garrison with grain. With this further excellent result, all the Alemannic tribes along the Rhine had been brought back within the Roman orbit for the time being, and the campaign could be considered complete.

But when the new campaigning season arrived, the *caesar* decided to deliver a final blow to the Franks. Although the Franks would become the most successful and long-lived barbarian people – to the point of taking possession, with Charlemagne, half a millennium later, of the western part of the Roman Empire under the aegis of the Church – they too required the formation of a confederation, although its origin is less well documented than the Alemannic one. The Romans had first faced the Franks (whose name derived from the Nordic *frekkr*, meaning daring or brave) under Gallienus, exactly a century before the Battle of Argentoratum, probably as a grouping of different populations – including the Chamavi, Bructeri, Amsivarii, Cattuarii, Cattii and Sicambri – that had settled on the middle and lower Rhine. Subgroups within the Franks later emerged, the most important of which were the Salii and the Chamavi: Gennobaudus was their first king to conclude a *foedus* with Rome. By this stage, the Roman army was full of Franks. In the period of the Tetrarchy, the emperors' campaigns had made use of units of Frankish auxiliaries. Silvanus, Magister Peditum of Constantius and then a usurper, was a Frank, as well as the son of a high-ranking officer, Bonitus, who had reached lofty heights under Constantine. A first phase of infiltration into the Roman armed forces was followed by colonization of the virtually abandoned fringes of the empire; Constantine himself had installed several groups in Gallia Belgica.

Generally less dangerous and less restless than the Alemanni, since Constantine had inflicted heavy defeats on them and slaughtered their chiefs in the games in Rome, the Franks had opted to take advantage of the difficulties which the empire seemed to be facing before the confederation under Chnodomar, and resumed their raiding. A band of 600 Frankish warriors penetrated into the valley of the Meuse, pillaging and looting. Thus, although the season had already turned, Julian opted once again to avoid entering winter quarters, and instead made for Colonia Agrippinensis (Cologne), preceded by Severus.

Achilles agrees to release Hector's body in return for its weight in gold – a scene from the *Iliad*, Villa Romana del Tellaro, Sicily. Achilles' armour, just visible at centre, reflects Roman military accoutrements from Julian's age. He wears the so-called 'Achilles costume' sported by triumphant emperors: muscled cuirass, gilded ridge helmet topped with a peacock feather (*toupha*) and white *thoracomacus* (leather undercuirass) with white and purple *pteryges* (defensive skirt). (Dipartimento dei beni culturali e dell'identità siciliana; authors' photo)

The arrival of the Magister Equitum obliged the barbarians to withdraw into two abandoned forts, one of which may have been in the centre of modern Maastricht. Severus laid siege to them and, when Julian's force arrived, the *caesar* made the blockade even more stringent by patrolling the Meuse at night with soldiers on boats, who were forced to break the forming layers of ice on the water, in order to prevent the Franks from escaping beyond the river. After that, he did not need to launch any assaults against the walls of the two strongholds: he merely waited for the besieged to surrender out of hunger and fatigue, which resulted at the end of January AD 358, after fifty-four days of siege – just before an army of Frankish comrades arrived to rescue them, so Ammianus informs us.

Julian sent the booty from his latest victory to the emperor and only then considered military operations to have ended, escorting his army into winter quarters in Lutetia (Paris). Such a long and fruitful campaign was something of a novelty for the empire, which had for many years only undertaken defensive actions on the Rhine border. In ten months of military activity, Julian, in only his second year of command, had obtained a clear victory

Detail of the helmet of Achilles, from the weighing Hector scene from the *Iliad*, Villa Romana del Tellaro, Sicily. (Dipartimento dei beni culturali e dell'identità siciliana; authors' photo)

over an army superior to his own, had reiterated Roman sovereignty over the Alemanni by leading his army into their territories beyond the Rhine, and stemmed the ambitions of the Franks in the area of modern Belgium. It would be many years before any Roman *caesar* or *augustus* could boast of having achieved similar results.

Another innovation concerned precisely the choice of Lutetia as the new Gallic capital, in place of Lugdunum (Lyon). The latter was now too far behind the border to be able to control any movements by invading forces. Following the same principle that had forced the emperors, for the past 100 years, to choose places nearest to the borders as imperial residences, Julian opted for a city closer to Lorraine and Belgium, where the military roads allowed rapid access to the most often threatened territories. In addition, the fertile plains of the Seine offered great opportunities for provisioning the army and Lutetia, sited on an island along the river, offered a degree of protection from enemy assault.

THE PACIFICATION OF GAUL

Despite the exceptional results achieved in the campaign of AD 357, the consolidation of the Rhine border was still a distant goal. Julian devoted himself to it with tireless alacrity, without paying too much attention, at least at first, to the scant recognition that came from Constantius' court, where too many people were interested in belittling his successes and casting him in bad light in the eyes of the (intrinsically suspicious) emperor.

In the campaign of the following year, Julian decided to free the Lower Rhine from the threat of raiding by the Salii and Chamavi, in order to allow the supply of the border forts using the river flotilla that transported grain from Aquitaine. Having decided that the proposal by the Praetorian Praefect

Fiorentius to buy peace with gold was neither viable nor worthwhile, Julian took up arms again in the second half of April AD 358, when the effects of the severe winter were still to be seen all around. He restricted the grain reserves to 20 days, made them into hardtack, and marched northwards at the head of an army against the Frankish Salii. During the rebellion of Magnentius, the latter had moved from their former base on the eastern bank of the Rhine, on the Lippe, into present-day North Brabant, and had taken full control of Batavia and of all of Toxandria, east of Antwerp.

In this campaign, too, Julian's action proved to be brilliant. He appeared on the chessboard when the barbarians still believed him to be in Lutetia (Paris) awaiting the grain convoys from Aquitaine. The Franks could do nothing other than agree to meet him in Atuatuca (Tongeren), where the *caesar*, intimidating them with an imposing deployment of his forces, led the negotiations, showing himself to be open to the idea of leaving the occupied lands in their hands. Then he dismissed them with a wealth of gifts, declaring himself ready to await their return to make a treaty. However, when they departed, he instead ordered a pursuit of them, sending Severus along the Rhine to cut off their retreat. When they saw themselves surrounded, the Franks offered their submission and Julian accepted, becoming the latest allies of the empire.

It was now the turn of the Chamavi, who had been beaten by Constantius Chlorus and settled in Gaul as colonists, but who then took advantage of the Salii movement to occupy their vacant territories and migrate south, also taking possession of lands west of the Rhine. With them Julian was more drastic, slaughtering most of them and forcing the survivors to flee across the river. Julian was helped in this task by a barbarian called Charietto, who attacked them on his behalf, forcing them out of their hiding places and obliging them to show themselves to the Romans, who had no difficulty in putting them to the sword. When their king then came begging before him, Julian put him to the test by ordering him to give his son as a hostage to guarantee the peace. The man replied to him with tears in his eyes that he had lost him in the war, and only at that moment did the *caesar* call the boy out from a mass of prisoners and presented him to his father. The *regulus* was so overjoyed, it is said, that he also handed over his wife as a hostage to Julian.

With the victory over Salii and Chamavi complete, the north-eastern frontier could be considered stabilized and this enabled Julian to reactivate communications with Aquitania for the transportation of wheat. For this purpose, he set up a fleet of 600 boats in less than ten months, using timber from the Vosges forests, and finally resumed the supply of not only the garrisons of the forts, but also the populations of those areas reduced to starvation after years of raiding and warfare.

However, as in the previous year, there was still space for another expedition, this time against the Alemanni once more. It is difficult to establish, according to the sources, whether it happened at the same time as the one against the Chamavi or immediately after the conclusion of the latter. There were in fact two kings, Suomarius and Hortarius, who had participated in the Battle of Argentoratum and had managed to escape in the aftermath. Julian crossed the Rhine again at Borgogetomagus (Worms), and attacked the territory of Suomarius first; despite the defection of his loyal Severus, who suddenly lost his nerve and became ineffective, the Alemannic king did not even try to oppose Julian: he immediately rushed to meet him

Detail from the weighing Hector scene from the *Iliad*, Villa Romana del Tellaro, Sicily. Interestingly, the simpler helmet design sported by Odysseus, on the left, is surmounted by a central crest and, on the top at the front, two small plumes in a V-shape, similar to the Cornuti helmets on the Arch of Constantine in Rome. The figure the artist based Odysseus on could have been a high-ranking officer of the Cornuti, possibly a tribune. (Dipartimento dei beni culturali e dell'identità siciliana; authors' photo)

and made his submission. Julian forgave him, provided that he returned any prisoners taken and he supplied the Roman troops on request.

Julian then moved further south to deal with Hortarius. Leaving Charietto behind, he managed to evade sections of road blocked by logs by taking more circuitous paths, which eventually led him to the inhabited and cultivated areas. Hortarius appeared only after the Romans had devastated the crops and set the villages on fire, and he too made an act of submission, that forced him to provide manpower and material necessary to rebuild the Gallic cities destroyed in his raids. Julian also found a way to extort from Hortarius all the prisoners that the king was trying to avoid giving back. The *caesar* had prepared for the meeting by gaining information from those soldiers who had already been freed, and recording the names of their companions still in Alemannic hands. When the king returned the few prisoners he had brought with him to Julian's control, Julian showed him the names on the registers of his secretaries and then he read aloud the names of those not yet returned. The barbarians imagined that some divine entity had informed the leader and hastened to return all of them to him.

However, this expedition against the two *reguli* was a mere show of force by Julian, which did not solve the problem of the Alemanni once and for all. But winter was upon him, and among the troops, who had been paid with little regularity, things were stirring; the sudden change of attitude on the part of Severus was a symbol of the difficulties which Julian was facing, caused by the parsimony with which his cousin spared him money. Julian therefore was forced to return to Lutetia (Paris), from where, waiting to resume operations, he visited the cities that had suffered the most raids, and made plans to rebuild the barns and warehouses destroyed. The forced collaboration of Suomarius and Hortarius, who according to the agreements provided manpower and materials, allowed the restoration and rebuilding of Castra Herculis (Doorenburg), Quadriburgium (Qualburg), Tricensimae

Julian's subjugation of the Rhine tribes, AD 357–60

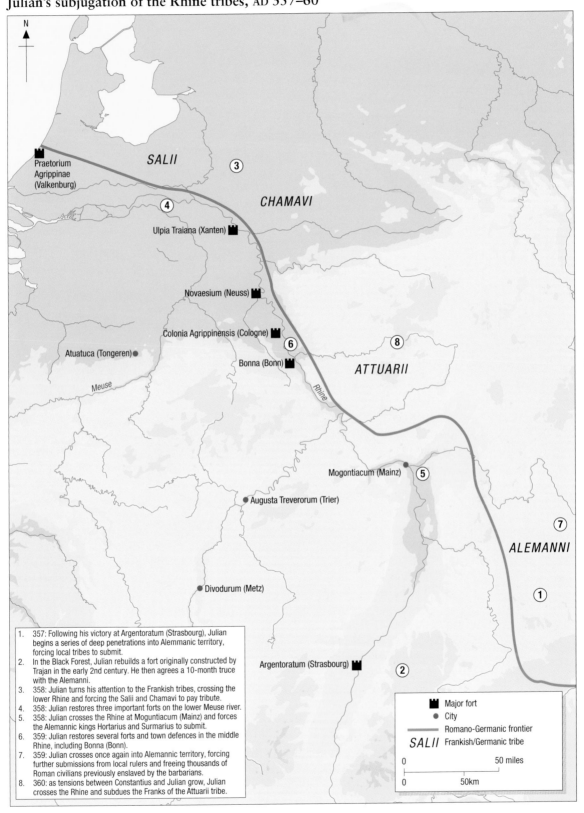

N

SALII

CHAMAVI

③

④

Praetorium
Agrippinae
(Valkenburg)

Ulpia Traiana (Xanten)

Novaesium (Neuss)

Colonia Agrippinensis (Cologne)

⑥

⑧

Atuatuca (Tongeren)

Bonna (Bonn)

ATTUARII

Meuse

Rhine

Mogontiacum (Mainz)

⑤

Augusta Treverorum (Trier)

⑦

ALEMANNI

Divodurum (Metz)

①

1. 357: Following his victory at Argentoratum (Strasbourg), Julian begins a series of deep penetrations into Alemmanic territory, forcing local tribes to submit.
2. In the Black Forest, Julian rebuilds a fort originally constructed by Trajan in the early 2nd century. He then agrees a 10-month truce with the Alemanni.
3. 358: Julian turns his attention to the Frankish tribes, crossing the lower Rhine and forcing the Salii and Chamavi to pay tribute.
4. 358: Julian restores three important forts on the lower Meuse river.
5. 358: Julian crosses the Rhine at Moguntiacum (Mainz) and forces the Alemannic kings Hortarius and Surmarius to submit.
6. 359: Julian restores several forts and town defences in the middle Rhine, including Bonna (Bonn).
7. 359: Julian crosses once again into Alemannic territory, forcing further submissions from local rulers and freeing thousands of Roman civilians previously enslaved by the barbarians.
8. 360: as tensions between Constantius and Julian grow, Julian crosses the Rhine and subdues the Franks of the Attuarii tribe.

Argentoratum (Strasbourg)

②

Major fort
City
Romano-Germanic frontier
SALII   Frankish/Germanic tribe

0   50 miles
0   50km

A

B

C

E

D

Coins minted during the reign of Emperor Julian, AD 361–363, showing the different types of armour he wore.
a) Lamellar (*squama*), Bronze 'AE19' (Heraclea mint)
b) Scale armour (*squama*)
c) Armour made of small metallic bosses, possibly applied on fabric (*thorax*), Centenionalis (Heraclea mint)
d) Scale armour (*squama*)
e) Mail armour (*lorica*)
(Private collection; authors' photo)

(Xanten), Novesium (Neuss), Bonna (Bonn), Antennacum (Anbdernach) and Binigum (Bingen). Meanwhile, on his behalf the tribune Ariobaudes was preparing the ground for a new campaign, ahead of the army.

In the spring of AD 359, when Julian's army set out, it had a new Magister Equitum, Lupicinus, who had replaced the recently deceased Severus. The Alemanni, however, had gathered on the other side of the Rhine to prevent Julian's force from passing and it was only thanks to the collaboration of Suomarius that Julian managed to disperse this threat. The barbarian chief invited the princes and the other rulers to supper in their village, while a flotilla of 40 boats carried 300 Roman soldiers south of the point provided for landing. Once on the other side, the raiders attacked the group of Alemannic dignitaries as they returned to their homes, slaughtering their retinue. Julian was now able to build a bridge of boats unmolested and engage in new devastation, which extended 15 miles east of the river, almost up to the territory of the Burgundians.

This show of force led to the submission of two other rulers, the brothers Macrianus and Ariobaudes, who had settled along the Middle Main. Immediately afterwards, further Roman devastation procured the deed of loyalty of Urius, Ursicinus and Vestralpus, who returned other prisoners. The empire was at last implementing a non-defensive strategy for securing Gaul. Julian's aim was to create a security belt immediately east of the Rhine, with a protective belt of allies that cushioned the pressure from the fiercest barbarian tribes immediately behind them, like the Burgundians and Saxons. The emperor Probus had already done this a century before, pushing the border beyond the Neckar, but then the frontier had been brought back along the Rhine due to pressure from the Alemanni. Having succeeded with infinitely inferior means compared to those which the empire possessed at the time of Probus, this was a source of great pride for Julian.

Within two years of Julian's epic victory at Argentoratum, which Zosimus compares to Alexander's victory at Gaugamela against the Persians, Gaul could be said to have returned under the full control of Rome, and the wounds caused by the continuous invasions appeared to be healing. Julian could feel satisfied that he had not only emulated Julius Caesar, who in his *Commentarii* had boasted of having ferried the Roman eagles twice over the Rhine, but had even surpassed him, leading his armies across on three occasions. Julian's personal assessment of his time in Gaul, based on his message to the Athenians (273–274), is as follows:

> It would take too long to enumerate everything and to write down every detail of the task that I accomplished within four years. But to sum it all up: Three times, while I was still Caesar, I crossed the Rhine; 20,000 persons who were held as captives on the further side of the Rhine I demanded and received back; in two battles and one siege I took captive 10,000 prisoners, and those not of unserviceable age but men in the prime of life; I sent to Constantius four cohorts of excellent infantry, three more of less quality infantry, and two very distinguished squadrons of cavalry. I have now with the help of the gods recovered all the towns, and by that time I had already recovered almost 40.

His work, later sustained by the conspicuous emoluments that his successors would pay to the barbarians, would restore a fragile peace to tormented Gaul. The next outbreak of hostilities of proportions equal to the one which had preceded his arrival would arise more than a decade after his victory, when the emperor Valentinian I suspended the subsidies to the Alemanni.

EMPEROR JULIAN

Over time, Julian became increasingly impatient with his subordinate status to his cousin, which prevented him from fully realizing his programs, especially of a religious nature. With his unrestrained admiration for the glorious past of Rome, the *caesar* had developed a sincere devotion to the ancient gods, now neglected in favour of Christianity, which above all the members of the ruling family were duty bound to follow. Moreover, he was not allowed to choose his closest collaborators, who were instead all men of his cousin; the councillors of the court nurtured the natural distrust of the sovereign, making him jealous of Julian's successes and causing him to distrust Julian's ambitions. They denigrated him as 'he who is a goat, not a man', because of his pointed beard, 'talented mole', 'Victorinus', 'ape dressed in purple' and 'Greek intellectual', and accused him of 'embellishing with well ornamented words his exploits that did not deserve it'.

The two cousins continued to endure each other until Persian pressure forced Constantius, at the beginning of AD 360, to request troops from his cousin. This did not comprise the four cohorts of infantry, three legions and two squadrons of cavalry that had been taken from him to that point: his request foresaw the transfer of the Auxilia Palatina of the Heruli, Batavi, Petulantes and Celti, as well as 300 men chosen from each legion, and the most valiant among the Scutarii and the Gentiles. His initiative, forwarded not directly to Julian but to his subordinates, triggered a series of misunderstandings that led the *caesar* to echo the discontent of the troops, who did not wish to leave their families to move to the East, as well as their calls to have him proclaimed *augustus*. No doubt, although there were many reasons to increase the strength of the Eastern army against the threat posed by the great king Shapur, to disband the Rhine border units would have induced the Franks and Alemanni to immediately rise up, nullifying Julian's five years of work.

Although undecided, Julian allowed himself to be raised up on a shield, in the barbarian manner, as had happened to Constantine the Great, and crowned with the necklace of the Draconarius of the Petulantes. Julian then proposed a division of the empire to his cousin – which would become the norm only a few decades later – offering to send troops recruited from among the peoples he had reduced to obedience, without depriving the territories of the soldiers guarding them. Constantius felt his sovereignty too threatened to take into consideration any proposed agreement, and bided his time, chiefly because he could not immediately abandon the Persian front and prepare the ground for civil war. The Alemanni resumed their attacks on the Rhine border at this point, and a short while later Julian came into the possession of a letter from King Vadomarus, addressed to Constantius, which referred to himself as 'your disobedient Caesar'. It was thought that the emperor had fomented the raids of the Alemanni to trouble his cousin; in any case, Julian managed to capture Vadomarus, putting an end to the threat. The death of Julian's wife Elena in the course of this year, who may have been poisoned by the empress, cut the final bonds between them and dispelled any scruples between the two antagonists.

At the beginning of AD 361, Julian dismissed the Praetorianus Praefectus appointed by his cousin, who had refused to declare loyalty to him, and resolved to march towards the East; not to bring troops to Constantius, but to attack him before he was himself attacked, while the emperor still had most of his troops in the East. Seeing that his cousin was taking possession of all the routes of communication between East and West, the emperor lost no more time and immediately organized advanced guards to block Julian's advance, and then moved towards Julian; but in Tarsus he caught a fever that forced him to stop, and poor weather worsened his condition. Constantius died on 3 November AD 361, in Mopsucrene in Cilicia, avoiding a dramatic civil war that would have dealt a terrible blow to the empire's resources, already damaged by losses and invasions. Later it was said that, on his deathbed, Constantius had designated Julian as his successor, which is possible, if we consider that, whatever he thought of his cousin, he was the only surviving male in the Constantine family in line.

Julian apparently wept at the news of his death, as Caesar had cried when he heard of that of Pompey the Great, but Julian did not delay in making for Constantinople, where he offered public condolences. The body of his cousin was buried beside his renowned father, thus sanctioning his assumption of power as a single emperor. No longer bound by his subordination to

Constantius, the young sovereign began to execute his three main objectives with zeal and fervour: the restoration of paganism to emulate the great emperors of the past; legislative reforms, imitating Marcus Aurelius, the philosopher emperor who inspired him; and finally a great expedition against Persia, to equal that of Alexander the Great. These acts would allow Julian to consider himself an emperor at the height of his powers.

But it was the expedition against Persia that obsessed him most, in so much as to induce him to neglect the advice of his collaborators, who warned him about the difficulties of the enterprise. He prepared the campaign in Antioch, where he arrived in the summer AD 362, leaving it in March of the following year, at the head of the last great expedition of conquest in the history of the Roman Empire. He feigned an advance on the Tigris, but instead marched along the Euphrates to Ctesiphon, in front of which he won a battle that did not allow him, however, to capture the city. Then he continued to advance into a region transformed into wasteland by the Persians, who tormented the Roman columns with increasingly devastating attacks, cutting off the supplies of the invaders. Julian, however, had committed the fatal error of burning the fleet to prevent it from falling into the enemy's hands. In the course of a further battle, the emperor learned that the rear-guard had been attacked, and rushed to its aid. In a hurry, he forgot to don his armour, and was hit in the ribs by a spear; we will never know whether it was thrown by a Persian warrior, a Saracen mercenary or a fanatical Christian from within his own army. Julian died in his tent after a brief agony, on 27 June AD 363, declaring: 'At the height of glory I deserved this distinguished departure from the world.'

It is said about him that he lived in the wrong period and that he died before being remembered as a tyrant. He certainly was motivated by good intentions, but there were too few collaborators who favoured him, and everything he tried to create dissolved at his death. This included the defence of Gaul, which within half a century would be invaded and occupied by the most diverse peoples, with whom Rome would have to come to terms, granting them the possession of entire provinces, or a third of the conquered lands, in exchange for an uncertain military support.

A *solidus* minted by Julian as Augustus in Constantinople, AD 361–63, from a private collection. The obverse shows a bearded Julian with the inscription: FL(AVIVS) CL(AVDIVS) IVLIANVS PP [Pater Patriae – 'father of the nation'] AVG [Augustus – 'Emperor']. (Heritage Auctions, HA.com)

THE BATTLEFIELD TODAY

The Battle of Argentoratum was fought on a plain at the edge of the Rhine Valley, near the village Oberhausbergen, to the west of Strasbourg. Hatt and Schwartz, after a very careful study, have changed the old hypothesis that considered the battle to have been fought west of the locality denominated Hill 175 near Oberhausbergen, and identified the battlefield as south of Oberhausbergen village. Hill 175 could have been the locality where at the beginning of the battle the Alemanni camouflaged their positions and established scouts. The fact that the barbarians were seen from this hill by the horsemen of Severus, the news that the Roman baggage train was being ambushed, and finally the indication that the baggage train guards were the first to notice the defeat of the enemy and then joined the battle, are all circumstances pointing to the fact that the battle was not fought west of this locality, but in the east and in the plain south of the present village of Oberhausbergen. The plain is visible today, is easily accessible and offers a clear sight of the possible battle array of both armies. To visit it, follow the D228 road from Hurtigheim or the N4 motorway from Ittenheim, taking the exit towards Oberhausbergen. The area of the plain is more and less in front of the sports and cultural centre of the village.

The battlefield today, looking east from behind the Roman lines during the battle, towards the place where the Roman cavalry clashed with the Alemanni. (Jasper Oorthuys © Karwansaray Publishers)

SELECT BIBLIOGRAPHY

Ancient Sources

Aulus Gellius, *Noctes Atticae,* in *Attic Nights*, LCL, HUP, Vol. III, Books 14–20, 1927

Ammianus Marcellinus, *The Histories–Res Gestae*, Latin text and English translation by J. C. Rolfe, Loeb Classical Library, 3 vols. London, 1939–50

Ammianus Marcellinus, *The Later Roman Empire (A.D. 354–378)*, ed. and transl. by Hamilton W., Suffolk, 1986

Aurelius Victor, *Livre des Césars*, traduction et commentaires par Pierre Dufraigne, Paris, *Les Belles Lettres*, 1975 (2003)

Caesar, *Gallic Wars*, ed. Otto Seel, Leipzig, 1961; LCL, HUP, Vols. I–III, 1917–2001

CIL, *Corpus Inscriptionum Latinarum*, vol. XIII *Inscriptiones trium Galliarum et Germaniarum Latinae*, pars I, fasc. 2 *Inscriptiones Belgicae*, Hirschfeld O. and Zangemeister C., Berlin, 1904

Dio Cassius, *Dio's Roman History*, 9 vols. with an English translation by Cary E., London, 1914–1927

Julian the Emperor, *Works*, Vol 2, ed. Wright W. C. F., Heinemann W., Cambridge: Harvard University Press, 1913

Julian, *Letter to the Athenians*, trans. W. C. Wright, Cambridge: Harvard University Press, 2002

Julian, *Complete Works*, Hastings, 2017

Libanius, *Funeral Oration for Julian*, trans. Norman A. F., Cambridge: Harvard University Press, 1969

Livy, *History*, 13 vols. with an English translation by B.O. Fister. Cambridge: Harvard University Press, 1926–43

Notitia Dignitatum, accedunt Notitia Urbis Constantinopolitanae et laterculi Provinciarum, O.Seeck (ed.), Berlin, 1876

XII Panegyrici Latini, ed. Baehrens E. Teubner, Lypsia, 1874

Panegyrici Latini, *In praise of later Roman Emperors. The Panegyrici Latini, introduction, translation and historical commentary*, ed. Nixon C.E.V. and Rodgers B.S., with Latin text of Mynors R.A.B., Berkeley and Los Angeles, 1994

Panégyriques latins, éd. E. Galletier, Paris, Les Belles Lettres, 1949–55

Tacitus, *Histories*, ed. Koestermann E., Vols. I–II, Lipsiae, 1957–69

Zosimus, *New History*, London, 1814, Book 3

Zosimus, *Histoire nouvelle*, éd. F. Paschoud, 2e éd., Paris, Les Belles Lettres, 1979–2000

Modern works

Alföldi, A., 'Cornuti: A Teutonic Contingent in the Service of Constantine the Great and its Decisive Role in the Battle at the Milvian Bridge', in *Dumbarton Oaks Papers*, 13, 1959, pp.169–79

Banck, A., *Byzantine Art in the Collection of the USSR,* Moscow, 1966

Barker, P., *The Armies and Enemies of Imperial Rome,* Worthing, 1981

Bayard D. and Massy L., 'Amiens romain. Samarobriva Ambianorum', in *Revue Archéologique de Picardie*, 1983, p.247

Benoist-Méchin J., *L'imperatore Giuliano*, Milano, Rusconi, 1979

Bidez J., *La vie de l'empereur Julien*, Paris, 1930

Blockey, R.C., 'Ammianus Marcellinus on the Battle of Strasbourg, Art and Analysis in the History', in *Phoenix*, 31, 3, autumn 1977, pp.218–31

Bowersock, G.W., *Julian the Apostate*, London,1978

Bouffartigue, J., *L'empereur Julien et la culture de son temps*, Paris, 1992

Browning, R., *The Emperor Julian*, London, 1975

Brulet, R. 'La militarisation de la Gaule du Nord au Bas-Empire et les petites agglomérations urbaines de Famars et de Bavay', in *Revue du Nord*, tome 77, no. 313, 1995, *Archéologie*, pp.55–70

Cascarino, G., and Sansilvestri C., *L'esercito romano: Armamento e organizzazione, Vol III, dal III secolo alla fine dell'Impero d'Occidente*, Rimini, 2009

Crawford, P., *Constantius II: Usurpers, Eunuchs and the Antichrist,* Barnsley, 2016

Delbrück, H., *History of the Art of War Within the Framework of Political History: The Germans*, Vol. II, Greenwood, 1980

Drinkwater, J. F., *The Alamanni and Rome (213–496)*, Oxford, 2007

Elton, H., *Warfare in Roman Europe AD 350–425,* New York, 1996

Frediani, A., *Le grandi battaglie di Roma Antica*, Rome, 2002

Geffcken, J., *Kaiser Julianus*, Leipzig, 1914

Goldsworthy, A., *Roman Warfare*, Cassell, New York, 2000

González, J.R., *Historia de las Legiones Romanas,* Madrid, 2003

Gundel, H. G, 'Der Keil in der germanischen Felschlacht', in *Gymnasium*, 50, 1939, pp.154–65

Hartley, E., Hawkes, J., Henig, M., and Mee, F., *Constantine the Great: York's Roman Emperor,* York, 2006

Hatt, J.J. and Schwartz, J., 'Le champ de bataille de Oberhausbergen', in *Bulletin de la Faculté des lettres de Strasbourg*, no. 42, 1963, pp.427–34

Head, C., *The Emperor Julian*, Twayne, Boston, 1976

Hoffman, D., *Das spatrömische Bewergunsheer und die Notitia Dignitatum*, Düsseldorf, 1970

Jelusić, M., 'Zu einem Schildzeichen der Notitia dignitatum. Neubewertung einer Grabmalerei mit der Darstellung des spätantiken Soldaten Flavius Maximianus aus der Villa Maria-Katakombe in Syrakus (reg. Siciliana/I)', in *Archäologisches Korrespondenzblatt*, Jahrgang 47, 2017, Heft 4, pp.513–32

Jerphagnon, L., *Julien dit l'Apostat*, Seuil: Paris, 1986

Lammert, F., *Die römische Taktik zu Beginn der Kaiserzeit und die Geschichtschreibung*, Leipzig, 1931 (*Philologus Supplementband*, 33, 2)

Lammert, F., 'Compte rendu de Schenk 1930', in *Gnomon*, 10, 1934, pp.271–74

Lammert, F., 'Phalanx', in *Paulys Realencyclopädie der classischen Altertumswissenschaft*, XIX, Stuttgart, 1938, col. 1625–46

Lammert, F., 'Der Keil in der Taktik des Altertums', in *Gymnasium*, 51, 1940, pp.15–31

Leguilloux, M., *Le cuir et la pelleterie à l'époque romaine*, Paris, 2004

MacDowall, S., *Late-Roman Infantryman 236–565 AD*, Osprey Publishing, London, 1994

MacDowall, S., *Late-Roman Cavalryman 236–565 AD*, Osprey Publishing, London, 1995

Matthews, J.F., *The Roman Empire of Ammianus*, London, 1989

Miks, C., 'Studien zur römischen Schwertbewaffnung in der Kaiserzeit', in *Kölner Studien zur Archäologie der römischen Provinzen*, Band 8, Rahden 2007

Miks, C., *Ein spatromischer Depotfund aus Koblenz am Rhein: Studien zu Kammhelmen der späten Kaiserzeit*, Mainz, 2014

Murdoch, A., *The Last Pagan*, Sparkford, 2003

Pattier, L., 'Recruter ses ennemis pour gagner les guerres irrégulières: les barbares au sein de l'armée du Bas-Empire', in *Stratégique*, 2009/1, no. 93–94–95–96, pp. 109–27

Polymnia Athanassiadi-Fowden, *Julian and Hellenism*, Oxford, 1981

Potter, D., *The Roman Empire at Bay AD 180–395*, New York, 2005

Raddatz, K., 'Die Bewaffnung der Germanen in der jüngeren römischen Kaiserzeit', in *Nachrichten von der Akademie der Wissenschaften in Göttingen*, Göttingen, 1967, pp.1–18

Ross, C., *Roman Legionary AD 284–337: The Age of Diocletian and Constantine the Great*, Oxford, 2015

Sarantis, A., and Christie N., *War and Warfare in Late-Antiquity*, Leiden, 2013

Seager, R., 'Roman Policy on the Rhine and the Danube in Ammianus', in *The Classical Quarterly*, 49, no. 2, 1999

Simpson, C. J., 'Julian and the "*Laeti*'": A Note on Ammianus Marcellinus, XX, 8, 13', in *Latomus*, T. 36, Fasc. 2 (Avril–Juin 1977), pp. 519–21

Solari, A., 'La rivolta procopiana a Costantinopoli', in *Byzantion*, 7, 1932, pp.143–48

Steuer, H., 'Germanische Heerlager des 4.15. Jahrhunderts in Südwestdeutschland (?)', in Nørgård Jørgensen A. (ed.): *Military Aspects of Scandinavian Society in a European Perspective, AD 1–1300: Papers from an International Research Seminar at the Danish National Museum, Copenhagen, 2–4 May 1996*, Copenhagen, 1997, pp.113–22

Tougher, S., *Julian the Apostate*, Edinburgh University Press, 2007

Schlette, F., *Germanen, zwischen Thorsberg und Ravenna*, Leipzig, 1971

Sylvain, J., 'Les formations tactiques en éperon et en tenaille dans l'armée romaine', in *Mélanges de l'Ecole française de Rome, Antiquité*, tome 116, no. 2, 2004, pp.1001–38

Speidel, M., *Ancient Germanic Warriors: Warrior Styles from Trajan's Column to Icelandic Sagas*, Routledge, New York, 2004

Van Berchem, D., 'L'armée de Dioclétien et la réforme constantinienne', in *Publications de l'Institut archéologique de Beyrouth*, 56, 1952

Various, *Die Franken, Wegbereiter Europas, 5. bis 8. Jahrhundert*, Mainz, 1996

Warry, J., *Warfare in the Classical World*, London, 1980

Will, E., 'Amiens ville militaire romaine', in *Mélanges Louis Jacob, Revue du Nord*, 36, 1954, pp.141–45

Wrede, H., *Die spätantike Hermengalerie von Welschbillig: Untersuchung zur Kunsttradition im 4. Jahrhundert n. Chr. und zur allgemeinen Bedeutung des antiken Hermenmals*, Berlin, 1972

Wucherpfennig, J., 'Julian's Most Famous Fight: the Battle of Strasbourg AD 357', in *Ancient Warfare*, Oct/Nov 2007, pp.29–33

INDEX

Figures in **bold** refer to illustrations.

Agendicum (Sens), siege of 15
Alemanni 7, 11–12, 13, 15, 17, 23, 24–25, 27–28, 80, 81–82, 85–86, **87**, 88, 89, 90
see also Germanic forces
Ammianus Marcellinus 13, 19, 27, 29, 30–31, 32, 37, 38–39, 42, 43, 44, 45, 47, 48, 51, 53–54, 55, 61, 62, 83
Res Gestae 5
Arch of Constantine 34, 40, **52**, **53**, **54**
Argentoratum (Strasbourg), battle of 5, 16, 47, 48, 56–79
aftermath 80–91
background to 17–28, **26**
battlefield today **61**, **63**, **76**, **77**, 91, **91**
Chnodomar's breakthrough **64–65**, **66**
Chnodomar's surrender **72–73** (74), 75–76, 77, **78–79**
description of 56–57, 60–63, 66–67
German casualties 77
German forces, location of 75
Germanic charge against the Roman Primani shield wall **68–69** (70)
Germanic forces, retreat and slaughter of 67, 71, 75, 76–77, **78–79**
Julian's follow-on operations 80–84
location of Julian's army **71**
maps 56
opening moves **58–59**
Roman casualties 77
site of Roman camp **57**, 60
Ariobaudes 88
armour 29, 31, 41, **43**, 83, 88
neck guards **40**
see also helmets
Auxulia Palatina **20–21** (22), 33–34, 40, 42–43, **52**, **53**, **54**, **55**, 63, 90

Bainobaudes 19, **20–21** (22), 23, 31

Barbatio 17, **18**, 19, 23, 24, 25, 32, 51, 52
battle plans
Germanic 51–52
Roman 52–55
belts **23**, **27**, 50
Brocomagus, battle of (AD 356) 39
brooches (*fibulae*) **23**, 42
crossbow type **16**, **19**, **23**

campaign chronology 16
campaign origins 4–15
arrival of Julian 13–15, **14**
collapse in Gaul 11–13
Constantine's dynasty 8–11
Rhine Frontier 5–7
caps 24
Caracalla 7
Castellum Divitia **13**
Catacombs of Villa Maria, Sicily **11**
Chamavi 38–39, 82, 84, 85, 87
Charietto 39
Charudes 7
Chnodomar 5, 12, 13, 25, **26**, 27, 32, 44, 45, 51, 52, 53, 56
breakthrough at Argentoratum **64–65**, **66**
imprisonment and death 80
physical appearance **32**
surrender of **72–73** (74), 75–76, 77, **78–79**
Christianity 4, 8, **8**, 11, **11**, **44**, 89, 91
Chrysopolis, battle of (AD 324) **6**
clothing 42, **42**, **81**
embroidery **25**
Roman sleeve **17**
coins **9**, 41, **82**, **88**, **91**
comitatenses 9, 33, 36, 37, **39**
commanders
Germanic 32, **32**
Roman 29–31
Constans 9, **10**, 16
Constantine II 9, **10**, 16
Constantine the Great (AD 306–37) 5, **6**, 7, **9**, 36, 37
dynasty of 8–11
rise of **6**
Constantius 9, 11, 12–13, 16, 19, 27–28, 51, 80

death **6**, 90
relations with Julian 89–90
Constantius Chlorus 8, 9

Dalmatius 9, **10**
Diocletian **6**, 8, 36

Flavius Claudius Iulianus (Julian) *see* Julian
Flavius Magnus Magentius *see* Magentius
foedus 7, 82
fortifications 13, **14**
Franks 7, 11, 13, 15, 82–83, 85

Galerius 6, 8
Gallus 9, 11, 16
Gaul
Julian's arrival and campaign 13–15, **14**
organization of Roman forces 36–37
pacification of 84–89, **87**
Rhine frontier, breakdown of 11–13
Germanic battle plans 51–52
battle array 52
Germanic forces 44–50, **48**, **49**
Alemannic military organization 45–46
casualties at Argentoratum 77
cavalry 52, **58–59**, 62–63
size of 44–45
tactics 46–49
war cries 63
weaponry 49–50
grave goods **23**

Hannibalianus 9
helmets 50, 53, 55, 86
christograms 8
Dunpantele-Intercisa type **39**
horns 40, **54**
neck guards **40**
ridge helmets **33**, **34**, 37, 40–41, 83, 84
spangenhelm **72–73** (74)
see also armour
horses 47, 56, 60, 76
Hortarius 85, 86
hunting **4**, 5, 42, 75

Iliad 83, 84, 86
intelligence 39

javelins *see* weaponry
Julian 4–5, 11, 12–13, 16, 17
  acclaimed *augustus* 77, 90
  approach to Argentoratum
    26, 27–28
  armour 31
  arrival and campaign in Gaul
    13–15, **14**
  at the Battle of Argentoratum
    56, 57, 61–62, 77
  birth 16
  as commander 29–31
  death 29, 91
  as Emperor 29, 89–91
  follow-on operations after
    Battle of Argentoratum
    80–84
  Letter to the Athenians 28
  *Letter to the Senate and People
    of Athens* 13
  military knowledge 29–30
  pacification of Gaul 84–89, **87**
  physical appearance 29, **29,
    30, 81, 82, 88, 91**
  prepares Auxulia Palatina of
    the Cornuti Seniores for a
    German raid **20–21** (22)
  relations with Barbatio 23–24
  relations with Constantius
    89–90
  reputation 25, 27, 29, 30, 89, 91
  tactics 38
Julius Caesar 4

Koblenz **15**

Laeti 19, 34, 36, **44**
  relations with Julian 23–24
Lepontius **43**, 44
Libanius 5, 24, 44, 53
Licinius 6, 8
limitanei 9, 33, 36, **39**, **43, 44**
Lupicinus 88
Lutetia 84

Macrianus 45, 88
Magnentius **10**, 11–12, 16, 32,
  43, 51, 85
Marcellus 13, 15
Marcus Aurelius 7

Maxentius 6
Maximianus 8, **11**
military tactics
  Germanic forces 46–49
  pincer plans 17, **18**, 19, 39, 81
  Roman 38–39
  shield-wall formations 39, 48,
    63, **68–69** (70)
  wedge formations (*cuneus*)
    47–49
mosaics 5, 22, 40, 41, 42 75, 76,
  83, 84, 86
Mursa Major, battle of (AD 351)
  11

Notitia Dignitatum 34, 36

Oberhausbergen 52, 91

paganism 4, 11, 29, 89, 91
Panegyrici Latini VIII 19
Persia 9, 91
Polymnia Athanassiadi-Fowden 29
Primani **42**, 43, 55, **64–65**, 67,
  68–69 (70)
prisoners 7, 85, 86
Probus 7, 89

Quadi 7

ripenses 33, **44**
Roman battle plans 52–55
  Roman order of battle 53–55
Roman Empire 4, 5, 7
  Constantine's dynasty 8–11, **10**
  Nerva–Antonine Dynasty
    (AD 96–192) 8
  Tetrarchy 5, 8, 9, 40, 82
Roman forces 33–43
  barbarus 7
  casualties at Argentoratum 77
  Catafractarii 28, 37, 38, 43,
    52, 55, **58–59**, 60, 62, **62**
  cavalry 19, 28, 33, 37, 38, 39,
    42, 43, 47, 53, 55, **58–59**,
    60–62, **62**
  comitatenses 9, 33, 36, 37, **39**
  fiscus barabarus 7
  infiltration by Franks 82
  limitanei 9, 33, 36, 37, **39**,
    43, 44
  organization in Gaul 36–37
  pacification of Gaul 84–89

prisoners as auxiliary troops 7
Roman military system 33–36
Sagittarii 28, 43
size of, at Argentoratum
  42–43
standard bearers **82**
tactics 38–39
weaponry 40–42, **42**
Roman towers, at Argentoratum
  (Strasbourg) **7**, **12**
Roman walls, Augustomagus
  (Senlis) **12**

saddles 76
Salii 39, 82, 84, 85, 87
sarcophagus 4
Serapio 32
Severus 6, 30–31, 39, 53, 57, 67,
  83, 85, 86
shields **11**, **20–21** (22), 41, **43,
  45**, 50, 50, **72–73** (74)
  bosses 35
  shield-wall formations 39, 48,
    63, **68–69** (70)
Silvanus 12, 13
Strasbourg *see* Argentoratum,
  (Strasbourg), battle of
Suebi 7
Suomarius 85–86, 88
swords *see* weaponry

Teutoni 7

Vadomarus 90
Valentinian 19, 23
Villa Romana del Tellaro, Sicily
  5, 22, 40, 41, 42, 75, 76, **83,
  84, 86**

war cries 63
weaponry
  Germanic forces **45, 47, 49–50,
    50, 68–69** (70)
  javelins 41, **47**, 49, 56, 57, 63,
    66, 71
  Roman forces 40–42, **42, 43**
  scabbards 36
  shafted weapons 41, **47**
  swords 36, 38, 41, 48, 49

Zosimus 62, 77, 89
  Historia Nova 5